# HANUMAN CHALISA

## (A Spiritual Experience)



Dr. Sandeep Kumar Sharma

DIAMOND BOOKS

www.diamondbooks.in

| | | |
|---|---|---|
| **Publisher** | **:** | **Diamond Pocket Books (P) Ltd.**<br>X-30, Okhla Industrial Area,<br>Phase-II, New Delhi-110020 |
| Phone | : | 011-40712200 |
| E-mail | : | wecare@diamondbooks.in |
| Website | : | www.diamondbooks.in |
| Edition | : | 2025 |
| Printed By | : | Repro (India) |

**HANUMAN CHALISA: A SPIRITUAL EXPERIENCE**

Author - *Dr. Sandeep Kumar Sharma*

***Dedicated to Lord Rama Devotee Hanuman***

Jai Shri Ram Jai Shri Ram Jai Shri Ram Jai Shri Ram Jai Shri Ram
Jai Shri Ram Jai Shri Ram Jai Shri Ram Jai Shri Ram Jai Shri Ram
Jai Shri Ram Jai Shri Ram Jai Shri Ram Jai Shri Ram Jai Shri Ram
Jai Shri Ram Jai Shri Ram Jai Shri Ram Jai Shri Ram Jai Shri Ram

# Publisher's Note

In India, Hanumanji and Hanuman Chalisa are known by heart to everyone. From their childhood till their last breath, crores of people, when they wake up in morning, sit and read Hanuman Chalisa in their temple or when they are in any sort of trouble or danger. By making Hanumanji happy, you can easily reach Lord Rama. This is blind faith, and devotion is always a dedication.

***Guru Gobind Dau Khade, Kaake Laagu Paay***
***Balihari Guru Aapne Shri Gobind Diyo Bataay.***

***-Kabir***

**(When both Guru and God stand before me, to whom should I bow first? I bow to the Guru, for it is through the Guru that I have been shown God.)**

This is a spiritual reason. The other is scientific reason. Tulsidasji composed the *Ramayana*. In his illness, he had written *Hanuman Chalisa*. After writing 40 verses, he recovered completely. Hanumanji was blessed by both Shiva and Vayu. He can be as small as he can and as big as he wants to be. In *Ramayana*, the Rama-Ravana war was held under his patronage. He can both walk and fly which means he was a Superman.

All Indians who believe in Indian culture would like to read this book. After many meetings with the author, I requested him to write this book. After reading almost 3000 pages about Hanumanji, he wrote this book.

I am confident that you will like this. Give me your opinion and encourage your friends to read this.

*I dedicate this version to my revered mother*
*Smt. Ishwardevi & father Sh. Govindram ji.*
*Without whose blessings the journey of*
*publication wouldn't have been possible.*

–Narender Kumar Verma
nk@dpb.in

# Foreword

Hanuman has been worshipped in all three ages. He was a devotee of Shri Rama in Treta Yuga. He became the protector of Pandavas in Dwaparyug and now in Kalyug, He is Sankat Mochana (the reliever of troubles) to his devotees. This is why he is considered immortal. All over the world, Tuesday and Saturday are considered the day of His worship. In the evening Boondi is offered as Prasad. On Saturday, offering 'chola' (red clothes, sacred offering) to his statue is a tradition. Reading Hanuman Chalisa on Saturday lessens the bad effect of Sadhe Saati and Dhaiyya. There is a provision for worshipping Hanumanji on the auspicious day of Deepawali. Considered as Rudravatar of Shiva, he is also known as Bajrangbali, Pawanputra, Marutinandan, Kesarinandan, Mahavir, and so on.

In the whole world, devotees of Hanuman believe that chanting Hanuman Chalisa invokes the divine intervention of Hanumanji. He is one such deity, whose method of worship is not as specific as other deities. Throughout the world, the method of worshipping Hanuman is the same all over. Tuesday and Saturday are two days related to Hanumanji. There is no difference of opinion in this. People from all over the world put chola on Hanumanji. Other traditions are also the same.

Hanuman Chalisa is one of the very famous short devotional hymns written by Tulsidasji, a 16th-century famous poet, saint, philosopher and devotee of Hanuman in which the activities of

Pawanputra Hanumanji have been presented. Along with this, apart from Hanuman, there are many incidents related to Lord Rama in Hanuman Chalisa. Rama's personality has also been depicted in simple words. The life of Hanuman has been shown from early childhood to old age. 'Chalisa' means 'forty'. This hymn has forty verses. The introduction consists of two couplets.

In only a few sentences, Tulsidas ji has covered every story of Hanuman and Rama in depth. In addition, Hanuman Chalisa has also provided a place for Ravana and his brothers. Without Ravana, Rama is incomplete, and without Rama, Ravana is incomplete. The other stories in the Ramayana and Hanuman Chalisa will lose their significance if Ravana is eliminated. During my early years, my mother, grandmother, elder sisters, other family members, and the family priest told me several legends about Hanuman.

Now that I've made an effort to fully comprehend Hanuman Chalisa, I realize that it contains those stories. Even as we claim to remember Hanuman Chalisa, most of devotees are unable to comprehend and fathom its depth. The proverb, '*Ek anaar sau bimaar*' (one solution for many problems') is aptly applicable to Hanuman Ji. A single Bajrangbali opened the fortunes of thousands of people. Although Hanuman completes all of his tasks by reciting the name of Rama, he constantly eases his devotees' burdens if they just pronounce any of his names even once.

Hanuman Chalisa is written in Awadhi language. It explains Hanuman ji's personality, traits, courage, strength, and devotion. It is highly popular among the followers of Hanuman, Regularly chanting the Hanuman Chalisa is thought to bestow Hanuman's blessings. Devotees of Hanuman memorize it. The mind is aroused by contemplating its profound feelings, devotion, and vast knowledge. In North India, it's highly well-known and well-liked. The 39th stanza of the Hanuman Chalisa states that

Hanuman ji will bless the one who recites it with dedication. In addition to Hanuman ji's blessings, they will have the blessings of Sitaram ji's. Chalisa can be recited with a resolution if you desire to do so, or you can pray to Hanuman ji on your own without a resolution. Observing fast on Tuesday is much more beneficial.

The five-faced Hanuman Ji is mentioned in mythology. Panchmukhi Hanuman is the name of five-faced Hanuman ji. Five distinct manifestations of Hanuman are thought to shield their followers from various angles. Peace, wealth, and security are provided by the idol of Panchmukhi Hanuman. There are five faces of Hanuman: Hayagriva on the upward face, Hanuman on the east face, Garuda on the west face, Varah on the north face, and Narasimha on the south face. This isn't a sheer coincidence but logical. It has been mentioned extensively in the book.

After Brahma, Vishnu, Mahesh, Rama, and Krishna, Hanuman ji is the most revered deity in Sanatan Dharma. There is only one temple dedicated to Brahma ji worldwide, and Rama is far less well-known than Krishna. The nation has the most temples dedicated to Lord Shiva and Shivling. There are temples dedicated to Lord Krishna after this. Among the temples of the gods, Hanuman Ji's is ranked third. In addition, there are temples where idols of all the gods and goddesses are consecrated. Constructing joint temples in the residential areas of cities and metropolises has become customary. These are not the same as temples of goddesses.

Huge statues of Hanuman Ji are installed in many cities across the country. The Panchmukhi Anjaneya Swamy statue located in Bidanagere Basaveshwara Math in Karnataka is 161 feet tall. Jakhu temple is situated in the middle of the hills of Shimla, where the statue of Lord Hanuman is 108 feet tall. There is a statue of Sankat Mochan Hanuman in Karol Bagh, Delhi. Here, Hanuman is shown tearing his chest. This is also a huge statue.

The statue of Lord Hanuman in the Nalco temple in the quiet town of Damanjodi in Odisha is 108.9 feet tall. The statue of Hanuman Ji in Paritala Anjaneya temple in Andhra Pradesh is 135 feet tall. India's tallest and largest Hanuman statue is installed on the banks of the Vamsadhara River in the Srikakulam district of Andhra Pradesh. It is 176 feet tall. There is a 105-foot-tall marble statue of Hanuman Ji on the side of Nandura National Highway 6 in Maharashtra. Hanuman Dham situated on the Birasat Ghat on the banks of Khannaut River in Uttar Pradesh has a 100 feet tall magnificent statue of Lord Hanuman. Hanuman Temple in Agara in Bangalore has a 102 feet tall statue of Bajrangbali. A hundred-foot-tall statue of Hanuman is situated in the Chhatarpur area of Delhi.

It is to be noted that present-day astrologers and scholars recommend that you put a picture of a particular god or goddess at the main entrance of your house for the accomplishment of your work. Similar advice is given to reduce the effect of black magic. We worship Gods and Goddesses. They are not our 'watchmen'. Gods and goddesses have a place in the temple of the house. They are worshipped and adored. Pictures, statues or other signs of any deity should not be installed at the main entrance of the house.

The objective of this book is to convey the deep secrets related to Hanuman Chalisa to the Hanuman devotees in simple words. No place has been given to misconceptions and interpolations in the book.

My heartfelt gratitude to Shri Narender Verma Ji, chairman of Diamond Books, for showing interest in the publication of this book.

-Dr. Sandeep Kumar Sharma

# Contents

# The Spiritual World of Hanuman Ji

Hanuman Ji and spirituality have a deep connection. He is considered the giver of nine Nidhis (treasures). These Nidhis are a symbol of material and spiritual prosperity. Hanuman Ji is a symbol of strength and health. Reciting *Hanuman Chalisa* cures both mental and physical diseases. Hanuman Ji is considered an incarnation of the powerful concept of resolving dilemmas and thinking ahead. He boosts his devotees up to face difficulties and emerge victorious. By the grace of Hanuman Ji, self-confidence enhances in a person and fear, anxiety and uncertainty end. Worshiping Hanuman Ji increases self-confidence, removes fear and anxiety and brings happiness and peace in life. Hanuman Ji is considered a god of intelligence and expansion.

The word 'Hanuman' is a combination of two Sanskrit words, 'Hanan' (destruction) and 'Man' (mind). It indicates a person who has conquered his ego. We deeply revere Hanuman. Before knowing his spirituality, we have to understand what spirituality is.

## Spirituality

You often hear the words *aadhyatma, aadhyatmik* and *aadhyatmikta* (self, spiritual and spirituality). What is the meaning of these words? How much depth is there in these words? Why is spirituality important for every person? Is it necessary to be spiritual? Many such questions come to everyone's mind.

The simple meaning of spirituality is: "To connect with and experience something bigger than yourself. It is not related to any religion, sect, philosophy, etc. Therefore, we can definitely say that spirituality means a way to adopt a different perspective on life. What could be the perspective? Spirituality frees us from dependence on material things. It helps in understanding the purpose of life. It teaches how to deal with change or uncertainty. Not only this, spirituality gives rise to positive emotions like peace, awe, satisfaction, gratitude and acceptance. This speeds up the process of personality development.

When a person moves towards spirituality, some changes are seen in him. The one who imbibes spirituality sees a part of the supreme power in all the creatures of the universe. He starts considering himself responsible for his sorrow, anger and suffering. He starts working for the welfare of all. This is the science of spirituality.

Saints and religious speakers explain the meaning of spiritual as the union of God with the soul.

Spirituality involves a sense of connection. It is distinct from religion. It is an inner path that enables a person to discover the essence of his or her being. Spiritual practices, including meditation, prayer, and contemplation are intended to develop a person's inner life. Spirituality is often experienced as a source of inspiration or guidance in life.

## Spiritual Path

In a wide variety of cultural and religious conceptions, spirituality is often seen as embracing a spiritual path that a person walks to achieve a certain goal, such as a higher level of awareness, deeper knowledge, or oneness with God or creation. A spiritual path can be thought of as a short-term path directed toward a specific goal, or a lifetime journey. Every event in life is part of the journey but may include particular pivotal moments or defining moments.

## Religion

Spirituality and religion can refer to the quest for the infinite or God. Scholars see the two as having different meanings. Religion is only one of the ways to experience spirituality. Religion is not the same as spirituality, but in civilization, spirituality takes the form of religion.

Those who talk about spirituality outside the religion often define themselves as "spiritual but not religious" and usually believe in the existence of many different spiritual paths. They emphasize the importance of finding one's path to spirituality.

## Spirituality is the source of infinite joy

Being spiritual means that a person knows from his own experience that he is the source of his joy. Spirituality is related to the inner life of man and it begins with his inner journey. All those activities that make a man refined, pure, full of joy, and give a feeling of completeness — all come under spirituality. The wise-men say that 'the vast is contained in the void and this vastness also contains the void. The one, who can understand this vast form of God and experiences it while living in this body, is spiritual.

## Personal Well-being

Prayer has attracted the attention of behavioural scientists in keeping with a general growth of interest in spirituality and complementary and alternative therapies.

If spirituality is understood as the search for inner peace or the basis of happiness, then some kind of spiritual practice is essential to personal well-being. This activity may or may not involve belief in a transcendental being. If a person has such a belief and feels that connection to such a transcendental being is the basis of happiness, then spiritual practice will be pursued on that basis. Even if a person does not have such a belief, spiritual practices are necessary for managing and understanding thoughts and feelings that would otherwise impede happiness. Many techniques developed and explored in religious contexts, such as meditation, are themselves extremely valuable as skills for managing aspects of inner life.

Ancient evidence suggests that Hanuman's spiritual guru was the Sun God. Matang Rishi and Narada Deva were also considered by Hanuman as his gurus. In many stories, Vasishtha Muni is also shown as Hanuman's Guru. It seems that Hanuman gained knowledge from experts in all subjects because he had a deep interest in his characteristics. He wanted to master all subjects like devotion, selfless service, gentleness, faith, courage, knowledge, compassion and strength and his character shows that he was proficient in all the subjects of that time. Like a person with all virtues, Hanuman is disciplined and maintains complete self-control. He is humble and loving. All these qualities are necessary to be spiritual.

Hanuman is considered an ocean of knowledge. He is endowed with wisdom, knowledge and eight siddhis. This is the reason he is God not only in Treta Yuga and Dwapar Yuga but also in Kali Yuga. The simple meaning of the word Vanar is - 'one who lives in the forest'. The word Vanar is made up of two words - 'Van' and 'Nar'. Apart from this, many meanings of the word Vanar have been given. The word Vanar also means monkey. It also means a caste of people living in the forest. In Ramayana, Vanars help Rama defeat Ravana. This is the reason why Vanars are usually depicted as human-like monkeys or human-like creatures. Hanuman is shown as a very strong man with the face of a monkey. He has a sacred thread hanging from his shoulder. Hanuman is shown with a bare body wearing only a *langot* (a loincloth).

Hanuman also received nine Nidhis from the Sun God and it is said that to study he would walk in front of the Sun God at the same speed as his chariot. The person who possesses the nine Nidhis has many miraculous qualities. These "Nav Nidhis" represent nine types of divine treasures or wealth which Hanuman Ji bestows upon his devotees in the form of both material and spiritual abundance. These Nidhis symbolize the blessings and grace that can be obtained through the devotion of Hanuman Ji.

### Mahapadma Nidhi

This treasure is earned in a satvik way. It contains wealth and material comforts and its effect lasts for seven generations. A person endowed with this Nidhi has strong religious feelings and the ability to give charity.

### Padma Nidhi

This Nidhi is a treasure of knowledge and wisdom. It is obtained through trade and its holder has a mixture of both Sattva and Raja Gunas.

### Mukunda Nidhi

Mukunda represents the treasure of divine grace and blessings. It represents the power of positive emotions and compassion and contributes to emotional well-being.

### Nanda Nidhi

It is a symbol of divine protection and represents the power to overcome negativity and obstacles.

### Makar Nidhi

Makar represents fertility and creativity. It signifies the human ability to generate new ideas, think innovatively and engage in artistic endeavours.

### Kacchapa Nidhi (turtle treasure)

A person keeps his wealth hidden in this Nidhi. The turtle protects itself under its shadow. It represents the stability, patience and flexibility required to deal with the challenges of life.

### Shankha Nidhi

It is the power of communication. The ability to express oneself. The person is fluent in speech.

### Kunda Nidhi

The Kunda is a symbol of illumination and knowledge. Scientifically, it is associated with self-discovery and the pursuit of knowledge.

### Kharva Nidhi

Kharva symbolizes the treasure of all kinds of material wealth and prosperity which includes precious gems, gold and abundance in all aspects of life.

Hanuman Ji is well-versed in all the nine Nidhis mentioned above. This indicates his spirituality. One who follows the ideals of Hanuman Ji becomes free from all kinds of negative energies.

### Removal of Negativity

You can easily remove negative energies, evil spirits and harmful influences by reciting Hanuman Chalisa. Reciting Hanuman Chalisa acts as a protective shield around you. Hanuman Ji is a powerful protector.

### Freedom from Fear

Devotees can overcome their fears, doubts and anxiety. Hanuman Chalisa is especially beneficial in stressful situations as it calms the mind and brings inner peace and stability. It strengthens spirituality. Daily recitation of Hanuman Chalisa unlocks your inner strength and resolve, enabling you to face life's obstacles with courage and fortitude.

### Remove Sins

Hanuman Chalisa helps in clearing accumulated bad karma or sins of the past by purifying the mind, heart and soul. Its daily recitation removes the burden of past karma and promotes positivity.

### Concentration

It increase focus and concentration because Hanuman Ji is the symbol of discipline and concentration. Regularly reciting Hanuman Chalisa helps in daily work and increases focus and concentration. It is beneficial for students.

### Spiritual Knowledge

Devotes can easily please Lord Rama by worshipping Lord Hanuman. People can get the blessings of Lord Rama and Lord Hanuman by reciting the Chalisa daily.

### Inner Strength

The verses of Hanuman Chalisa promote inner purity by purifying your emotions and thoughts. It aids in getting rid of undesirable qualities like jealousy, greed and anger and increases your inner strength and you can easily control your senses.

### Courage

It makes you strong and courageous. Courage and confidence can only be gained by worshipping Lord Hanuman. You can gain protection and power. By chanting Hanuman Chalisa, you can become strong and powerful.

## Spiritual Benefits of Reciting Hanuman Chalisa:

### Blessing for Health

Lord Hanuman is associated with strength and health. It is believed that reciting Hanuman Chalisa cures both mental and physical illnesses.

### Free from Constraint

Reciting Hanuman Chalisa helps to remove obstacles in your personal and professional life; it makes your life free from constraints.

### Pleasant Feeling

It is believed that reciting the Chalisa before sleeping helps people sleep well and removes nightmares.

### Destroyer of Evil Powers

Reciting Hanuman Chalisa makes you strong, courageous and brave to fight all evil forces.

### Tantra-Mantra

If you ever feel that you are suffering from the effects of black magic, then you are advised to recite Hanuman Chalisa daily.

### Hanuman and Bhakti Yoga

Hanuman is the epitome of devotion. He is the only deity among the Sanatan deities who is devoted to another God. Hanuman's devotion to Rama is unimaginable to us. He has no ego. He does everything possible to serve Rama, but never sees himself as the doer. He lives only to dedication and devotion. Hanuman shows us his commitment and dedication in all the selfless acts he does for Rama. For him, there is nothing else but his commitment to the one he loves the most.

There is an episode at the end of Ramayana when Ram and Sita discuss their importance and tell Hanuman about his role as a devotee. Their union was possible only because of him. His love is the glue that holds everything together.

Hanuman is also known as a semi-god — half human and half monkey. Because of his human-like qualities, it is easy to understand, identify and feel close to Hanuman. In Sanatan symbolism, the monkey symbolizes the human mind, which is always restless and never still.

As an incarnation of Vishnu, Hanuman is known as the pinnacle of human perfection, representing the asanas or physical practice of yoga. He created the asana series Surya Namaskar. He is also the son of Vayu, who taught him the science of pranayama, or 'breath control'. Hanuman taught pranayama to humans.

To surrender yourself completely to God, to serve Him lovingly according to His mood, inspiration or command, to give Him constant pleasure and to expect nothing in return — these are the form of devotion. All these things are found in the character of Hanuman. He considers his body, mind, intellect, strength, discretion, feelings, abilities, time, etc. to be only of God and keeps them engaged in the service of his Lord Rama.

The feeling of giving happiness to God with devotion and love is called 'Rati'. It is mainly considered to be of four types. These are:

*i. Dasya Rati,*

*ii. Sakhya Rati,*

*iii. Vatsalya Rati, and*

*iv. Madhurya Rati.*

## Dasya Rati

Dasya Rati is the initial step of Bhagwad Bhakti. In this Rati, the devotee considers himself as the servant's servant and and serves his Lord with the feeling of a servant. A true servant is one who neither has any attachment towards his belongings, body, mind, intellect, etc. nor has the slightest pride in serving. He understands that whatever he is offering comes from the power and inspiration of the deity he served.

Hanuman Ji is so skilled in understanding the feelings of Lord Rama that he renders the necessary service even before the thought arises in the mind of the Lord. Even before the Lord entered Lanka, he arranged for his stay and a safe place for his army camp, etc. He always keeps Lord at ease through his service skills. While going in search of Sita, he was only asked to bring news of Sita's well-being. There was no context of burning Lanka, but when he hears Trijata's dream in Ashok Vatika, quick-witted Hanuman performs the unique service of burning Lanka, taking it as Lord Rama's sign and inspiration.

## Sakhya Rati

After Dasya Rati, the stage of Sakhya Rati begins. When there is a sense of mutual equality between the devotee and the Lord, it is called Sakhya Rati. In this too, the main feeling is to give pleasure to the Lord. In Dasya Rati, the slave always has this hesitation that the master may be displeased with him or he may commit a mistake in front of him. These weaknesses do not exist in Sakha Bhava because in this all hesitation is destroyed and the sense of friendship remains strong. Then where is the question of mistakes? Here both of us are equal. Such belief becomes deeply rooted. Hence, the emotional intimacy of the Lord is attained more in Sakhya Rati than in Dasya Rati.

In 'Vibhishana Sharanagati' of Valmiki's Ramayana, there is a very vivid description of Hanuman Ji advising Lord Rama like a wise friend. Addressing the monkeys, Rama asks them, "Should Vibhishana be included or not? You all express your views on this matter."

Then Sugreeva, Angad, Sharabha, Maind, Jambvan and others expressed their views one by one. After all, Hanuman ji, the best among them and endowed with the knowledge of all the scriptures, spoke in sweet, meaningful, beautiful and brief words, "Maharaj Shri Rama! Whatever I will say, I will not say it out of debate or argument, competition, pride in being more intelligent or any kind of desire. I will say only what I consider to be true keeping in view the gravity of the task." Hanuman, while expressing his opinion, says, "In my opinion, it seems appropriate to include Vibhishana."

## Vatsalya Rati (love and affection)

It is considered superior to Sakhya Rati. In the feeling of love, the devotee does not consider himself equal to a friend. Rather, the way parents nurture their children, they worship God in the same way. As a rule, where there is affection for God, there must be an attitude of serving Him. Therefore, Vatsalya Rati, Dasya and Sakhya Bhaav are also included in secondary form. This is the reason why Hanuman Ji could not bear God walking on foot. Whenever God wanted to go somewhere, Hanuman Ji immediately took Him on his shoulders and set out. This is a unique example of service-oriented Vatsalya Bhava.

## Madhurya-Rati

In Bhakti scriptures, Madhurya Rati is considered to be even better than Vatsalya Rati. It is also called Kanta Rati. It has two types. These are:

*Swakiya Madhurya Rati* and
*Parkiya Madhurya Rati.*

Parkiya Madhurya Rati is proved to be the best because of self-sacrifice. Although to some extent there is some personal desire for happiness in this worldly love, in the spiritual world where the devotee is related to God, there is no smell of worldly lust in the devotee. He only desires to provide happiness to his beloved (God). Does he have any interest of his own? As if he no longer exists. As a result of such selfless feelings, Acharya has considered Parakiya Madhurya Rati as the highest supreme devotion.

In all the rituals described, each other is considered inferior or superior. A very mysterious thing in this matter is the Rati through which the seeker engages in devotion to God. If there is complete selflessness in it, then all-round perfection comes in that Rati, that is, there is no deficiency in that Rati in the least compared to any other Rati. Although Hanuman ji has Dasya Rati for God, it is not any less than Parakiya Madhurya Rati in any sense. Hanuman Ji is always eager to serve. For example – *Ram kaaj karibe ko aatur.*

Hanuman ji is always eager to serve like a very hungry and very thirsty person. Parakiya Bhava is superior because it does not have any selfish motive. Still, it does have partial self-will, and there is also the feeling of happiness. In this sense, Hanuman ji has crossed Parakiya Madhurya Rati to the extreme. He has no desire for himself except to serve Rama in every way and to give him happiness. The second thing is that no matter how high the love of the worldly Parakiya bhava, that is, even if she has no desire for sustenance from her husband, she still needs sustenance for her body etc., so this heroine has to arrange for food, clothes and other comforts, if not from her beloved, then from somewhere else. But Hanuman ji took the form of a monkey so that he never needs even the slightest thing from anyone. He does not need clothes, food, a house respect, fame, etc. A monkey survives in the jungle by eating fruits, flowers, leaves, etc. and by living on trees. In the worldly parakiya bhava, there is a familial relationship, but Hanuman ji has a relationship only with God. In this way, his Dasya Rati is very unique. It becomes even higher than Madhurya Rati.

Madhurya Rati can be divided into two parts based on the difference in parakiya situation. As -

*Sanyogavasthaparak* and *Viyogavasthaparak*

## Sanyogavasthaparak

All the literary scholars and philosophers have considered Viyog Rati to be better and more interesting than Sanyog Rati. Both natures are present in Hanuman ji in a very unique form. In Sanyog Rati, the wife stays close to the husband and serves him by providing him food, etc. When the husband goes abroad, that is, during the time of separation, she remembers and thinks about him. Hanuman ji serves Lord Rama completely during the time of union. When separated, he remains immersed in his worship and thoughts. He remains always absorbed in him. There is a wonderful uniqueness in his thoughts also. A faithful wife remains only engaged in remembering and thinking. *Rama charit sunbe ko rasiya.* Listening and talking about the life and qualities of the Lord has no limit. He has taken such a body and has also formed such a relationship with God that wherever and whenever Ram Katha is being told, Hanuman appears there freely. He experiences the sweetness of listening to the story.

Hanuman transcends everything. He does not want separation from his beloved Lord anywhere like a faithful wife from her husband and a devotee from God.

But Hanumanji's case is unique among all these. When God started going to his heavenly abode, then Hanumanji asked for this boon, "Lord! Kindly allow me to live here on this earth. Till the time your unending and most sacred story is being told on this earth, I will stay here and listen to it with utmost love."

Hanumanji's devotion speaks it all. Due to this, every aspect of his life is affected. The rising of the sea, burning of Lanka, bringing Sanjivani, killing of fierce demons, etc. are the shining examples of the service of Hanuman Ji. He is so devoted and careful in service that he does not miss even the smallest service like snapping his fingers when Ram Ji yawns. Hanuman Ji's skill in service is incomparable. He understands even the subtlest feelings arising in Ram Ji's mind and immediately renders the service accordingly. What to do when, how to do, how to behave with whom, etc., from the smallest event of life to the biggest event of war, all are not untouched by the effect and miracle of his Dasya Rati. Dasya Rati has worked like lightning in his entire life. In love and devotion, he even surpasses the pinnacle of detachment and selflessness. In this world, he was considered the omnipotent and the giver of eight Siddhis and nine Nidhis.

The activities, conduct, thoughts and behaviour of the great devotee Hanuman Ji are not only for Sanatan but are extremely beneficial teachings for all mankind. By studying them, every person can make his temporal and spiritual life successful. That is why Maruti Nandan is such a popular God for Indians. His followers and devotees and his temples are present in almost every village and town of India from Kashmir to Kanyakumari and from Dwarka to Jagannathpuri. Hanuman Ji is also very popular in foreign countries like Nepal, Malaysia, Indonesia, Japan, Java, etc. and his worship in various forms is prevalent there.

The personality of Hanuman Ji is extremely bright, philanthropic and amazing. His conduct, thoughts, feelings, qualities, character and every incident of his life are the door to salvation and prosperity for all mankind. There is a precious and golden combination of spirituality and behaviour in his life. Hanuman Ji's character is a moving confluence of karma, bhakti and knowledge. If someone dives into it, his welfare is certain.

Hanuman ji's nishkam-karmayoga or Dasya Rati is such a mysterious key that opens the locks of Shreya and Preya very easily. It is so complete, beneficial and beneficial that even today a human being can attain peace, satisfaction and culmination very quickly by being dedicated to this sadhana. God loves his servant very much. Lord Shankar knows this secret and that is why he incarnated in the form of Hanuman ji and presented a very grand and unique ideal of Dasya Bhakti by serving Lord Ram ji. The servant has to depend on the mercy of his Lord. He performs all his tasks under the shelter of that grace. He keeps looking towards the grace of the Lord. The shelter of the grace of God is the sign of exclusive devotion.

Hanuman Ji's exclusive devotion increases gradually. He sees his Lord present in every particle of the world and the universe. Once Lord Rama was sitting on the Peak of Subel Mountain with Vibhishan, Sugreev, Angad, Neel, Nal, Hanuman ji and others. in the clear moonlight. He asked everyone - "How is this dark colour present in the moon?" Everyone expressed their views. At last Hanuman Ji said -

***Kah Hanumant sunahu prabhu sasi tumhar priya daas.***
***Tav murati bidhu ur basti soi syamata abhaas.***

"Lord, listen, the moon is your devoted servant. Your beautiful form resides in the heart of the moon. The reflection of the same form is in it."

This answer of Hanuman ji is proof of his devotion towards Lord Rama. Lord Rama always resides in Hanuman ji's heart. He had shown proof of this to everyone by ripping his heart open. He sees only Him everywhere, inside and outside.

### Seva (Service)

Like exceptional devotion, the feeling of service is also fully developed in Hanuman Ji's life. Only he is exceptional, whose wisdom never wavers that he is a servant and the animate and inanimate world is the form of my lord. This characteristic of Hanuman ji is seen in his first meeting with his Lord Ram ji.

A servant or slave never moves anywhere else except his master and his only thought is the service of his lord. A servant's heart is always restless to serve his lord. As soon as he recognized his lord, Hanuman ji became ready to serve him. He could not see the separation and sorrow of his lord and he became worried about the search for Mother Janaki. He immediately requested, "Lord! The monkey king Sugreev lives on this mountain. He is your servant. Lord! Make friends with him. Make him fearless by considering him poor and hapless. He will search for Sita ji and will send crores of monkeys everywhere."

Having explained everything in this manner, Hanuman Ji was not going to miss the opportunity. How could he take his worshipper on foot? He immediately took both the brothers on his shoulders and took them to Sugreev.

The happiness and satisfaction of the master is the treasure of the servant. Hanuman ji gets extraordinary pleasure in serving. He serves for his happiness. He considers service as his ultimate self-interest, he gets happiness at every step in serving. He did not care about any terrible trouble that came upon him while bringing happiness to his master. Rather, he accepts the trouble, and adversity that came in the work of the Lord as the ultimate happiness. He embraces it to his heart.

An extraordinary quality of Hanuman ji is that despite being infinitely knowledgeable, adept in the arts of music, etc., incomparably strong and endowed with all virtues, he is always ready to do even the smallest service of his Lord. Even after achieving complete success in all the tasks of the Lord, this feeling always remains in his heart. Hanuman Ji is the ultimate ideal for loyal servants. Remembering him is extremely auspicious for everyone.

## Excellence in Devotion

In the Uttarakhand of Padma Purana, in support of the excellence of devotion, God has said to Narad - "Narad! I neither reside in Vaikuntha nor the hearts of Yogis. My true abode is where my devotees sing my praises. I am satisfied when the people worship my devotees with incense and flowers and this satisfaction is more worthy than I am worshipped. Those people, who listen to my Purana Katha, but criticize the songs of my devotees, deserve my hatred."

On attaining this extreme step of the path of devotion, the duality of the devotee dissolves and non-duality arises in him. The devotee attains oneness with God or liberation in life. But Hanuman ji considered devotion better than liberation. Mahavir Hanuman is a committed devotee of Dasharath's son Lord Rama and Janakanandini Sita.

When the demons of Lanka set fire to Hanuman's tail, Sita ji prayed to Abhi in extreme excitement and said- "O Abhidev! If my service to my husband is sincere, my penance is established and I have followed pure fidelity to my husband, then you become cool for the devotee Hanuman. Being the best friend of Hanuman's father Vayu and due to this prayer of Maa Sita, Agnidev became extremely cool and didn't let Hanuman's tail burn even a little.

## Yogic Siddhis

Yogic Siddhis are of eight types. These are: Anima, Mahima, Garima, Laghima, Prapti, Prakamya, Ishitva and Vashitva. All these eight Siddhis were fully established in the supreme devotee Hanuman ji. The clear form of each of these Siddhis is visible in the conduct of Mahavir Hanuman ji.

## Anima and Laghima

After crossing the ocean and killing 'Lankini', the nocturnal gatekeeper of Lanka, in the course of searching for Janakanandini, Hanuman ji assumes a very minute form and inspects the entire city of Lanka at night, according to Goswami Tulsidas. But due to his extremely subtle form, the residents of that place do not even know about him. Hanuman Ji had become completely invisible to the enemies. Reaching Ashok Vatika and sitting in the leaves of the Shishampa (sesame) tree, he introduces himself to Janaki Mata and describes the condition of Rama. Through these distortions, we get to know the full status of the two siddhis, Anima and Laghima, in Hanuman.

## Mahima (Glory)

In the face-off with Surasa while crossing the ocean, Hanuman gradually expanded his body from ten to almost a hundred yojanas. When Hanuman said, "Ram ji will come with the monkey armies and destroy the demon-clad Lanka in a moment," Janaki asked, "Oh monkey! You are of very small body and other monkeys and bears too must be of small body like you. Then how will they fight such strong and huge demons?"

When Sita expressed such doubt, he assured her and showed his immense power by making himself as huge as a golden rock. On both these occasions, his gradually increasing body was not able to fit into the infinite sky due to its hugeness. In these incidents, we get a clear glimpse of the established form of glory and success in Hanuman ji.

## Garima (Dignity)

Once Hanuman ji was lying with his tail spread in a part of Gandhamadana. At the same time, seeing the proud Bhimsen coming, he said to him laughingly, "Anagh! Due to old age, I am unable to get up myself. Please move my tail and go ahead."

Laughing in defiance, Bhimsen started moving the tail of that great monkey with his left hand. But it didn't move even a bit. Then he started applying force with both his hands. Still, that tail which was raised like a rainbow didn't move even a bit. Due to this unexpected defeat, Bhimsen recognized him and with an ashamed face, asked for forgiveness from that monkey-like person. This description clearly shows the full bloom of dignity in Hanuman.

## Prapti (Gain)

When the attainment of perfection is established, the seeker yogi gets the desired object. Many monkeys and bears were also sent in all directions in search of Sita. Maruti was one of them. He had only sincere and devout desire to see the mother. As a result, shortly after reaching Lanka, he suddenly got the desired sight of Janaka Nandini Mata in Ashoka Vatika and he was satisfied.

## Prakamya (power to obtain the desirable)

Once the prakamya siddhi is established, the object the seeker desires is soon available to him. The inner aspiration of devotee Hanuman was the achievement of inexhaustible devotion and accordingly, the all-pervading Lord Rama didn't consider himself completely successful even after giving that boon to the devotee.

## Ishitva (Divinity)

Hanuman was a successful commander who perfectly conducted the army of monkeys and bears of Lord Rama and was also a supreme devotee. Therefore, the prestigious form of Ishitva Siddhi is also directly visible in him.

## Vashitva

Once Vashitva is established, self-conquest is also automatically perfected in the individual. Hanuman was strictly celibate and completely self-controlled. Therefore, *atulit baldhama* constantly exists in them.

## Bal-Purushartha (effort of strength)

Maruti had immense physical, mental and spiritual strength. He was invincible to all beings, including gods, demons and humans. He was never defeated by anyone. He was never hurt though Meghnad had put them in bondage once. But there was something else that caused him to be captured. When Meghnad wielded the weapon given by Brahma, he got himself tied to it, to keep the importance of that Brahmastra. If he wanted, he would have neutralise that Brahmastra. But there were two reasons for not doing so, first, that if that weapon failed, the immense glory of the Creator of the universe would be erased, and second, the reason was to reach Dashanana by that bond and burn his city. There is no end to the intellectual strength and manliness of Hanuman. No one can know or limit his movement in the world. At the order of Jambavan, he brought the mountain containing medicine from the Himalayas. As a result, Rama, Lakshman and all the monkeys who had fainted from the use of those medicines became conscious again. Thereafter, the mountain was placed on the Himalayas. When Rama began to lament after Lakshman fainted, then, as per the order of Sushen, Hanuman again brought a mountain containing herbs from the Himalayas and Lakshman was healed by the use of its herbs. His strength is infinite. That is why no opponent can stand against him. He had also killed numerous monsters.

## Ram Bhakti (Rama devotee)

Hanuman's devotion to Rama is indescribable. Lord Rama himself became indebted to him. The almighty Lord was deeply mesmerized by his love and devotion. Rama said, "O Hanuman! You have located Sita, the daughter of Videha, and by telling good news about her you have righteously protected the entire Raghu dynasty and the mighty Lakshman and me today.

After the coronation of Rama, Sita happily presented a necklace of divine gems to Hanuman. With its brightness, the divine idol of Hanuman was illuminated with unparalleled beauty.

After wearing the necklace, Hanuman was so adorned as if a mountain was embellished with a garland of white clouds like a cluster of moon rays. Having found such a necklace, he began to search for the name of Rama in it too. Finally, he has made a divine glimpse of Rama in his heart. Then the Lord asked, "Hanuman! Do you love our name more than we do?" To this Hanuman immediately replied, "Lord! Your name is much better than yours. I say this with wisdom and certainty. You have only saved the inhabitants of Ayodhya, but your name always saves the three worlds."

This is Hanuman's devotion to Rama. Once Sri Ramachandra said to Sri Hanuman, "Hanuman! If you had asked me for something, my mind would have been very satisfied. So today, you must ask for something.

Hanuman folded his hands and prayed, "Lord Rajarajendra! May my supreme affection always remain at your lotus feet! O Sri Raghuveer! May my unwavering devotion remain in you alone! May there be no inner affection for me anywhere else except you. Please grant me this boon."

❐

# Evolution of Hanuman Chalisa

There came a time in the history of India when foreign invaders continuously attacked Hindustan and made unsuccessful attempts to end its existence. After this, Mughal emperor Babar established his supremacy. Despite this, no one could completely destroy the roots of Sanatan Dharma.

In the 16th century, saint-poet Tulsidas was a contemporary of Mughal emperor Akbar. He was an ardent devotee of Lord Rama. Keeping in view the then social and political conditions, Tulsidas ji accomplished a great task by writing the book *Ramcharitmanas* in Awadhi language, considered by many as the poetic retelling of the Sanskrit epic Ramayana by Valmiki. Tulsidas ji composed Hanuman Chalisa as a tribute to Hanuman. Hanuman is a powerful monkey god. He is an ardent devotee of Lord Rama. Hanuman Chalisa is written in the Awadhi language. Awadhi is a dialect of Hindi.

There is an interesting story behind writing Hanuman Chalisa. Tulsidas ji was a very popular and revered saint among the Sanatan Dharmis. His fame was spread far and wide in North India. Mughal emperor Akbar was told about this by his courtiers. Akbar's heart was filled with curiosity. He became eager to meet Tulsidas. Akbar called Goswami ji to his court. Various religious topics were discussed with Tulsidas ji. Impressed by him, Akbar said to Tulsidas ji- "Introduce me to your Lord Shri Rama."

Tulsidas ji said, "Lord Shri Rama appears before his devotees only."

Akbar became furious on hearing this. He put Goswami Tulsidas ji in prison. It is said that Goswami ji wrote Hanuman Chalisa in Awadhi language in this prison. As soon as the work of writing Hanuman Chalisa was completed, monkeys surrounded the entire Fatehpur Sikri and attacked Fatehpur Sikri. Mughal soldiers got worried on seeing innumerable monkeys. Akbar's soldiers tried their best to stop the terror of monkeys but they were not successful. Akbar got the information about this. Akbar consulted his ministers. The ministers advised him to release Tulsidas ji from prison. Akbar followed the advice of his ministers and released Tulsidas ji from prison. On seeing Tulsidas ji being released from prison, the monkeys left the entire area at the same time. Mughal emperor Akbar was surprised to see this. The news of this amazing incident spread like wildfire. After this, the glory of Goswami Tulsidas ji spread far and wide.

It was the influence of Sanatan Dharma that no foreign ruler could erase our religious and cultural heritage. Tulsidas ji composed Hanuman Chalisa and Ramcharitmanas and gave the message to the whole world that whoever tried to wage an undeclared war against Sanatan Dharma would be completely destroyed. Aurangzeb adopted the policy of demolishing temples and the Mughal Empire came to an end in no time. British rulers, learning from the mistakes of the Mughals, commercialized our religious, cultural and social beliefs but stuck in vicious cycle of money-making. As a result, their sunset started in such a way that to date the sunrise of their empire has not happened and will never happen because Hanuman is protecting India even today.

❐

# Features of Hanuman Chalisa

By reciting Hanuman Chalisa, a person gets courage, strength and positive energy. By reading it regularly, self-confidence and peace develop in the mind. By His grace, the obstacles in life are destroyed. Hanuman Chalisa has many features. After studying it, the following attributes are visible.

## Power and courage

Hanuman ji is considered a symbol of power and courage. He is "Anjani Putra" and "Pavansut". His bravery and strength have been glorified in Hanuman Chalisa. He goes in all four directions in search of Sita. He crosses the sea and reaches Lanka. He is happy to see Sita in Ashok Vatika. To give life to Lakshman, when he is unable to identify the Sanjivani herb, he lifts the mountain and brings it. This is a symbol of strength and courage.

## Knowledge and intelligence

He is considered a symbol of knowledge and intelligence. Making Ram and Lakshman, who were wandering in the forest, friends with Sugriva is a symbol of intelligence. When Sugriva gives information about the four directions, Hanuman uses his knowledge to search for Sita. He inspires devotees to face difficulties with patience and discretion.

## Devotion and service

Hanuman ji is the ultimate devotee of Shri Rama. Tulsidas ji has depicted this form in Hanuman Chalisa. Hanuman ji has also been shown as a Rama devotee in Maharishi Valmiki's Ramayana. He presented the highest example of dedication and service.

## Sankat Mochak

Hanuman ji relieves Rama and Lakshman from all their troubles. This is the reason why it is currently believed that by reciting Hanuman Chalisa, all the troubles of the devotee are removed, and they gain mental and physical strength.

## Spiritual and emotional benefits

Hanuman ji is a spiritual guru. Just as a guru paves the way for his disciples to reach God, in the same way, Hanuman imparts spiritual knowledge to his devotees. Reciting Hanuman Chalisa also provides spiritual knowledge and emotional benefits.

## Protection and courage

Hanuman is a symbol of strength. He is also considered a symbol of fearlessness. Hanuman ji is worshipped in these forms. One gets the courage to face the challenges of life. Therefore, it is believed that the regular recitation of Hanuman Chalisa gives a sense of security and courage. It drives away negative energy and fear.

## Mental peace and meditation

The rhythmic recitation of Hanuman Chalisa has a calming effect on the mind. It helps devotees to focus on their thoughts and goals and achieve mental peace.

## Overcoming obstacles

It is also believed that the regular recitation of Hanuman Chalisa helps in overcoming personal and professional obstacles. Hanuman helps devotees get out of difficult times. Provides solutions and guidance.

## Panchmukhi Hanuman (Five-faced Hanuman)

Ahiravana, Ravana's brother, was the king of Pataal Lok (realm below the earth). He was a powerful demon. After the killing of Meghnad or Indrajit, Ravana called Ahiravana from Pataal Lok to win the war. Ahiravana was a devotee of Brahma Ji, and he had also got a boon from Brahma that he would be killed only when someone would extinguish candles in 5 directions simultaneously. Vibhishan had warned Rama by telling him this. Ahiravana attacked Rama's camp many times, but he was unsuccessful. Hanuman Ji was deployed to protect the camps of both Rama and Lakshmana. After failing many times, Ahiravana disguised himself as Vibhishan and entered the camp of Lord Rama and Lakshmana when they were sleeping. Ahiravana took the sleeping Rama and Lakshmana to Pataal Loka. Hanumana got disturbed after not finding Rama and Lakshmana in his camp. Expressing doubt, Vibhishan said to Hanuman, "Yes, yes, Ahiravana has succeeded in his purpose. Probably he has taken Rama and Lakshmana to the underworld. You go there and see."

Following Vibhishan's advice, Hanuman reached Pataal Lok in search of Rama and Lakshmana. When Hanuman was sure that Ahiravana had brought Rama and Lakshmana to Pataal Lok, he assumed the Panchmukhi form to kill Ahiravana. Hanuman with five faces simultaneously extinguished five candles in all four directions. Thus, Hanuman killed Ahiravana and freed Rama and Lakshmana from Pataal Lok.

Panchmukhi Hanuman is a powerful and revered deity in Hindu mythology. The five faces — Hanuman, Narasimha, Garuda, Varaha and Hayagriva — provide unique blessings and represent different aspects of divine power and protection. It is believed that worshipping Panchmukhi Hanuman removes obstacles, evils and provides comprehensive guidance and help to devotees.

### Upper facing: Hayagriva

Panchmukhi Hanuman is considered to be the most powerful incarnation of Lord Hanuman. In this form, Hanuman's face is facing upwards. Hayagriva represents knowledge and wisdom. Hanuman is known for his wisdom and education among his devotees. By worshipping this face, the devotee succeeds in gaining spiritual knowledge. The knowledge is clear. When clear spiritual knowledge is attained, then the devotee can achieve success in the educational field.

### East Facing: Hanuman

East-facing Hanuman is a symbol of courage and strength. This form of Lord Hanuman is worshiped the most. This form shows Hanuman's devotion towards Lord Rama. It is believed that those who worship east-facing Hanuman have courage, confidence and protection from harm.

### West Facing: Garuda

The west-facing Hanuman in Panchmukhi Hanuman is Garuda. Garuda is considered to be the vehicle of Lord Vishnu.

This form of Panchmukhi Hanuman represents freedom and liberation. Protection from black magic and all kinds of poisonous influences is provided.

## North Facing: Varaha

The north face of Panchmukhi Hanuman is known as Varaha. It is the boar incarnation of Lord Vishnu. This face symbolizes the power of upliftment and restoration. The form of Varaha is related to the removal of misfortune and the restoration of lost wealth and prosperity. He is worshipped by devotees for his strength and ability to overcome any difficulty.

## South Facing: Narasimha

The south-facing Panchmukhi Hanuman is Narasimha, the half-man, half-lion incarnation of Lord Vishnu. This form of Lord Hanuman symbolizes protection from evil and the destruction of fear. Narasimha's fierce and powerful presence is believed to remove obstacles from his devotee's life and ensure protection from negative forces.

## Hanuman Chalisa in Daily Life

Anyone can recite Hanuman Chalisa with a sense of security. It is believed that reciting Hanuman Chalisa in the evening is beneficial to calm one's heart and to reflect on it. One can recite it before setting out on a journey. Reciting Hanuman Chalisa is also beneficial before starting a new job. There is no better way than this for success and security.

Hanuman ji is prominent among those people of the Mahabharata era who had the good fortune of making their presence felt even in Kaliyug. Today, even though we consider monkeys to be the counterparts of Hanuman, in Tretayug, Vanars (monkeys) were a community that lived like normal humans.

Yaksha, Daksha, Rakshas, Daitya, Danav, Sur, Asur, and others were human races. Similarly, Vanars were a race. Probably, the tail of this race must have been its biggest identity. Hence, Hanuman ji got a respected place among the gods and goddesses. Hanuman ji's act as a Sankat Mochak (one who relieves trouble) is unique, and even today, he is our troubleshooter. Just remember him with faith and devotion, and he will destroy all your troubles in a moment.

Jai Bajrangbali!

❐

# Hanuman Chalisa's Original Text

## Couplet (doha)

***Shri Guru Charan Saroj Raj, Nijman Mukuru Sudhari,***
***Varnau Raghuvar Vimal Jasu, Jo Dayaku Phal Chari.***

***Buddhiheen Tanu Janike, Sumirau Pavan Kumar,***
***Bal Buddhi Vidya Dehu Mohe, Harahu Kales Vikaar.***

## Quatrain (choupai)

*Jai Hanuman Gyan Gun Sagar |*
*Jai Kapis Tihun Lok Ujagar || 1*

*Ram Doot Atulit Bal Dhaamaa |*
*Anjani Putra Pavan Sut Naamaa || 2*

*Mahavir Vikram Bajrangi |*
*Kumati Nivar Sumati Ke Sangi || 3*

*Kanchan Varan Viraj Subesa |*
*Kanan Kundal Kunchit Kesha || 4*

*Hath Vajra Aur Dhwaja Viraaje |*
*Kaandhe Moonj Janeu Saaje || 5*

*Sankar Suvan Kesari Nandan |*
*Tej Prataap Maha Jag Vandan || 6*
*Vidyavaan Guni Ati Chaatur |*
*Ram Kaj Karibe Ko Aatur || 7*
*Prabhu Charitra Sunibe Ko Rasiya |*
*Ram Lakhan Sita Man Basiya || 8*
*Sooukshma Roop Dhari Siyahin Dikhava |*
*Vikat Roop Dhari Lank Jarava || 9*
*Bhim Roop Dhari Asur Sanhare |*
*Ramachandra ji Ke Kaaj Sanvare || 10*
*Laay Sanjivani Lakhan Jiyaye |*
*Shri Raghuvir Harashi Ur laaye || 11*
*Raghupati Keenhi Bahut Badhaai |*
*Tum Mam Priya Bharatahi Sam Bhai || 12*
*Sahas Badan Tumharo Yash Gaave |*
*As Kahi Shripati Kanth Lagaave || 13*
*Sankadhik Brahmaadi Munisa |*
*Narad Sarad Sahit Ahisa || 14*
*Yam Kuber Dikpaal Jahan Te |*
*Kavi Kovid Kahi Sake Kahan Te || 15*
*Tum Upkaar Sugreevahin Keenha |*
*Ram Milaaye Rajpad Deenha || 16*
*Tumharo Mantra Vibhishan Maana |*
*Lankeshwar Bhaye Sab Jag Jaana || 17*
*Yug Sahasra Yojan Par Bhaanu |*
*Leelyo Taahi Madhur Phal Jaanu || 18*
*Prabhu Mudrika Meli Mukh Maahee |*
*Jaladhi Langhi Gaye Achraj Naahee || 19*
*Durgam Kaaj Jagat Ke Jete |*
*Sugam Anugraha Tumhare Tete || 20*
*Ram Duwaare Tum Rakhvaare |*
*Hot Na Aagya Binu Paisaare || 21*
*Sab Sukh Lahai Tumhaari Sarna |*
*Tum Rakshak Kaahu Ko Darna || 22*

*Aapan Tej Samharo Aapai |*
*Teenon Lok Haankte Kanpai || 23*
*Bhoot Pisaach Nikat Nahin Aavai |*
*Mahavir Jab Naam Sunavai || 24*
*Nasai Rog Harai Sab Pira |*
*Japat Nirantar Hanumat Bira || 25*
*Sankat Se Hanuman Chhudavai |*
*Man Kram Vachan Dhyan Jo Lavai || 26*
*Sab Par Ram Tapasvi Raaja |*
*Tin Ke Kaaj Sakal Tum Saaja | |27*
*Aur Manorath Jo Koi Laavai |*
*Soi Amit Jeevan Phal Paavai || 28*
*Charon Jug Partaap Tumhaara |*
*Hai Parsiddh Jagat Ujiyaara || 29*
*Sadhu Sant Ke Tum Rakhware |*
*AsurNikandan Ram Dulaare || 30*
*Ashta Siddhi Nav Nidhi Ke Data |*
*As Bar Deen Janki Mata || 31*
*Ram Rasaayan Tumhare Paasa |*
*Sada Raho Raghupati Ke Daasa || 32*
*Tumhare Bhajan Ram Ko Pavai |*
*Janam Janam Ke Dukh Bisraavai || 33*
*Antkaal Raghuvar Pur Jaayee |*
*Jahan Janam Hari Bhakt Kahaayee || 34*
*Aur Devta Chitt Na Dharahin |*
*Hanumat Sei Sarv Sukh Karahin || 35*
*Sankat Kate Mite Sab Peera |*
*Jo Sumirai Hanumat Balbeera || 36*
*Jai Jai Jai Hanuman Gosaain |*
*Kripa Karahun Gurudev Ki Naayin || 37*
*Jo Shat Bar Path Kare Koi |*
*Chhutahi Bandi Maha Sukh Hoi || 38*

*Jo Yeh Padhe Hanuman Chalisa |*
*Hoye Siddhi Saakhi Gaureesa || 39*
*Tulsidas Sada Hari Chera |*
*Keejai Naath Hriday Mahn Dera || 40*

## Couplet

***Pavantanay Sankat Haran, Mangal Murati Roop |***
***Ram Lakhan Sita Sahit, Hridaya Basahu Sur Bhoop | |***

❐

# Explanation of Hanuman Chalisa Path

## Couplet (doha)

***Shri Guru Charan Saroj Raj, Nijman Mukuru Sudhari |***
***Varnau Raghuvar Vimal Jasu Jo Dayaku Phal Chari | |***

[I cleanse the mirror of my mind with the dust of the Guru's lotus feet. Then I sing the pure, unspoiled glory of Lord Rama, who bestows the four-fold fruits of life — *dharma, artha, kama, and moksha.*]

## The Essence

All the happiness of the world is present in the feet of the Guru. Even the dust of his feet can help in removing all our sorrows. Therefore, the blessings of the Guru make life happy. It invokes auspiciousness. If you seek the blessings of your Guru before starting any work, all obstacles automatically disappear. By doing so, the work attains auspiciousness. This is our very ancient tradition.

Following his ancient tradition, Saint Tulsidas ji started Hanuman Chalisa by seeking the blessings of Shri Guru. Here, there are two words: Shri and Guru. According to him, here Shri is the form of Guru, or Guru is empowered by Shri. The word 'Shri' is undoubtedly feminine. Therefore, here, the word Shri refers to Mother Sita. Mahants, saints, religious preachers, religious analysts, scholars and intellectuals accept Sita as the most important Guru in Ramayana. Mother Sita is considered a symbol of mercy and grace. It is described in Maharishi Valmiki's *Ramayana* that Rama never killed any demon in the presence of Sita. According to the narrator of Ramayana, Maa Sita forgave all those demons who deserved to be killed. Kakasur was the first to receive forgiveness from Maa Sita.

Hanuman ji's first meeting with Maa Sita was in Ashok Vatika of Lanka. He had not seen Maa Sita before this. Hanuman was very impressed by meeting Maa Sita. Hanuman ji learned a lot from this first meeting. Ashok means one who has no grief and Vatika means garden, orchard, etc. So the simple meaning of Ashok Vatika is such a garden, where there is no sorrow, anguish, grief and enmity of any kind. Seeing Maa Sita sitting under a tree in Ashok Vatika, Hanuman understood that a lot can be learned from her. Keeping these forms and qualities in mind, Tulsidas considered Sita in the form of a divine soul as his Guru and started composing Hanuman Chalisa with the desire of receiving blessings from her.

Tulsidas calls the feet of the Guru as lotus. The lotus is considered a sacred flower. Lotus grows in mud. It is offered to the gods and goddesses. So what message do we get here? Through the lotus, we learn that the Guru always solves all problems with a calm mind. He shows the way to remove negative facts so that the energy and environment around us can be positive.

Tulsidas wishes for the 'Saroj' i.e. dust of the Guru's feet. He believes that the dust of the Guru's feet has divine power. This dust has the power to clean his mind and eyes. By cleaning the mirror of the mind along with the eyes, Tulsidas will be able to see himself with Ram.

The academic Guru imparts knowledge of letters, and the spiritual Guru gives the vision of God. We should serve both the Gurus. Only by serving can we get the dust from the Guru's feet. When any person succeeds in doing this, he becomes attached to Guru Prem. Here, 'Prem' means to 'serve'. 'Serve' means to please. What will be the way to 'serve'? The way is to sit at the feet of your spiritual Guru and listen to him. Tulsidas ji here clearly wants to say that one should sit at the feet of Shri Guru and receive knowledge from him. This is love. This is a service. This is attachment.

In *'Barnau Raghuvar Bimal Jasu,'* Raghuvar means descendant of the Raghu dynasty. Here, Tulsidas ji tells through history that Rama belongs to the Raghu dynasty, and he is going to tell the glory of Lord Rama. We all know that Hanuman Chalisa describes the glory of Hanuman ji and his deeds. Then why does Tulsidas ji want to mention the name of Rama here? The reality is that Hanuman Chalisa contains the glory of Lord Rama. There is no existence of Rama without Hanuman and Hanuman without Rama.

Just as Ramayan cannot be imagined without Rama, Ravana cannot be imagined without Rama. Similarly, a deep study of the Chalisa makes it clear that whatever Hanuman does, he does for Lord Rama. Rama is hidden in everything he does. Saint Tulsidas has placed Hanuman and Rama at the center of Hanuman Chalisa. Readers are pleased to know that Rama and Hanuman are pleased to hear each other's glories. In simple words, Rama is most pleased when his devotee Hanuman is glorified, and Hanuman is most pleased when Lord Rama is glorified.

Man attains four fruits in life at the feet of Shri Guru. For a materialistic devotee, the four goals are: *Dharma, Artha, Kama and Moksha.* For Mukti, the four goals are *Salokya Mukti, Samipya Mukti, Sayujya Mukti and Sarupya Mukti*. For a person who seeks only devotion, there are four goals: *Dharma, Gyan, Yoga and Japa.*

❐

***Buddhiheen Tanu Janike Sumirau Pavan Kumar,***
***Bal Buddhi Vidya Dehu Mohe, Harahu Kales Vikaar.***

[O Son of Wind God! I remember you being aware of my low intelligence. Give me courage, insight, and knowledge of all types and take away all of my flaws and sufferings.]

## The Essence

Tulsidas ji politely prays to Rama's devotee and servant Hanuman ji: "Hey Pawan kumar, I'm mindless. I can't do anything without you. Please help me. At this moment, no one is with me apart from you." A disciple requests his Guru to guide him, fill him with knowledge, and lead him towards a spiritual life so that he can attain the supreme God. Just like that, Tulsidas ji also wants to gain spiritual knowledge and start his life.

Spiritual knowledge has the power to remove all the flaws from the human mind. Conscience and intellect can strengthen because spiritual weakness can give sorrow to a person, give pain, tempt and make you insensitive. In such a situation, humans get under their control. Here Tulsidas is trying to explain the importance of spiritual acceptance.

Just like the very fickle nature of monkeys, our minds are also fickle. It is not in the power of an ordinary person to keep the fickle nature of monkeys and the restlessness of the human mind serious for a moment. Only he can establish his dominance over both of them, who is familiar with the mentality of both.

Hanuman ji has learnt to control his own fickle nature. He has realized that a fickle nature makes anyone irrational and due to this he cannot do well to not only himself but to anyone in the world, so what is the benefit of such fickleness? Having mastered this knowledge, Hanuman became the chief of the monkeys. The monkey community respects him. Hanuman is a storehouse of all virtues. In simple words, Hanuman ji is proficient in behaving wickedly with the wicked and behaving gently with the gentleman. Due to this quality, Hanuman got the privilege of serving Shri Ram.

Tulsidas calls our and our shortcomings as Kalesh and Bikara. According to the Patanjali Yoga Sutra, there are five types of Kalesh. As-

- Avidya means bad perception, Avidya means ignorance. Ignorance does not differentiate between good and bad. Hence, ignorant people find faults even in good things. This should be avoided.
- Asmita means ego, an ignorant person loses his ego by gaining little knowledge. Then he is filled with ego. Due to this, he starts walking on the wrong path and fails to attain salvation.
- Raga means attachment or enjoyment, due to Avidya and Asmita, a person starts singing a different kind of Raga. In this Raga, enjoyment and luxury become important. He becomes selfish.
- Hatred means bad feeling, selfish people are always afflicted with hatred. Such people do not do any good to anyone. They have bad feelings for everyone.
- Abhinivesh means fear or insecurity. This is the reason why such people always feel insecure. They fear that anyone can harm them anytime, anywhere. Tulsidas ji teaches to get free from these five Kaleshas.

Like Kaleshas, Tulsidas ji also warns about bikara which refers to types of vices. These are also harmful for humans. Six types of vices have been described -

- Kama means lust or desires, which arise in the mind
- Krodha means anger, which arises from frustrated desires,
- Lobha means greed, which arises from unfulfilled desires,
- Moha means delusion, which arises from ignorance,
- Mada means pride, which arises from ego and
- Matsarya means jealousy/envy, which arises from ungratefulness.

It is not easy to deal with these five types of troubles and six types of vices in this mortal world because these eleven elements surround every human being. They disrupt knowledge and self-confidence. They are capable of destroying spiritual knowledge. The fickle mind of a human being seeks the joy of life only in pleasure and luxury. Spirituality makes things rule-bound while pleasure paves the way for free movement. Now who can tell that spirituality develops a human being in an all-round way and makes him free till he attains salvation? Hanuman is the best option for this. Being the eleventh Rudra, Hanuman is the most capable of helping us in removing these eleven defects. He is also a symbol of immense strength, intelligence and wisdom. Tulsidas ji has confirmed this in the entire Hanuman Chalisa. This is why Tulsidas tries to educate us ignorant humans by keeping himself at the center that he himself is praying to Hanuman ji to remove all his troubles and disorders and make life happy. Only when he would get freedom from these eleven greedy elements, will he be able to convey the teachings of Rama devotee Hanuman to you. This is why Tulsidas uses the word 'Tanu' here, which refers to the self or the body.

❐

## Quatrain (Choupai)

***Jai Hanuman Gyan Gun Sagar |***
***Jai Kapis Tihun Lok Ujagar || 1***

[Hail Hanuman ji, the ocean of knowledge and virtues. Hail the king of monkeys, who illuminates all the three worlds.]

## The Essence

*'Jai Hanuman Gyan Gun Sagar'* means Hanuman ji is the first among the learned. So what does it mean here? Its simple meaning is that in those times, education was given importance. The best learned people were given special respect in the society of that time. Hanuman ji is the leader among the learned because with the power of his intellect, he paved his way by removing the obstacles like Surasa, Lankini, and others from his way and got the good fortune of becoming the eternal companion of Shri Ram. Tulsidas ji has described our ancient education system through Hanuman Chalisa. In those times, all sections of the human community in Aryavart had equal opportunities to progress and study. Merit was given importance without any discrimination.

All the disciples were given education and training in social, economic, political, religious, cultural, natural, botanical, chemical, administrative, marine, community, warfare, science, universe, arms and ammunition, management, food, cuisine, entertainment, health, exercise, deceit and fraud, along with the creation, operation and destruction of 'maya'. Hanuman had obtained special qualifications in all these faculties and received the honour of the best student, which no other student has been able to achieve till date. Today we will find people with postgraduate degrees in many subjects. We will find people who know many languages. But we will not find a person as all-rounder and highly knowledgeable as Hanuman ji.

The speech of a prudent person reveals his personality. It reveals the level of his knowledge. It was through Hanuman's speech that Rama came to know how powerful Hanuman was. It was because of Hanuman's knowledge, wisdom and fearlessness that Rama not only allowed him to come closer to him but also entrusted him with important tasks. Tulsidas Ji made it clear through the first couplet of Hanuman Chalisa that the depth of knowledge and qualities inherent in Hanuman are capable of removing all our sorrows.

It is known from Maharishi Valmiki's Ramayana and other scriptures that Hanuman was a grammarian. He was proficient in Mimamsa because he didn't make any mistakes in the sentences. He was also proficient in logic. He didn't make any mistake in the words and sentences spoken by him. Hanuman Ji's body remains calm while communicating. Not only this, the listener is also listening to Hanuman with complete focus. This means that Hanuman Ji is speaking emotionally, meaningfully, seriously and according to the circumstances.

When Hanuman ji met Ram and Lakshman for the first time under Rishimukh Mountain, the words spoken by Hanuman won Rama's heart. This is the best example of Hanuman being knowledgeable. The distressed Ram and Lakshman listened to Hanuman's conversation with restraint and both became his admirers. Certainly, Hanuman ji's eloquence, sentence structure, choice of words and dialogue delivery must have been discussed between Rama and Lakshmana, that is why Rama told Lakshman that Hanuman is the ocean of knowledge and virtues. One meaning of this is that during the exile period, Rama did not meet anyone like Hanuman who uses words in such an effective way that the person in front gets enchanted.

Familiar with the academic ashram system, Rama guessed that Hanuman must have received the company of special teachers. Rama knows very well that the company of special teachers is given only to those disciples who have a sharp intellect distinguished from the other disciples of the ashram. Hanuman must have got a lot of time to study under expert gurus. Tulsidas tells us that the quality of Hanuman's dialogue reflects the quality of his education. Hanuman must have been as highly qualified as Rama. In Hanuman Chalisa, Tulsidas makes it clear that not a single fault was found in Hanuman's speech and in his body language. We all know that when a person speaks, his body language indicates the tenor of the words. Looking at the life story of Hanuman described in various scriptures, it would be apt to assume that Rama was confident that Hanuman had full command over the Vedas. Why? Because mastery over the Vedas manifested through expertise in various aspects of communication and self-expression. According to a section of subject experts, a person well versed in Atharva Veda has natural humility. Knowledgeable people say that humility is reflected in the words and gestures of the person. This humility indicates mastery over the Yajur Veda. According to linguists, grandeur in one's vocabulary and a great power is imparted by abundant study. Rigveda experts say that it gives the scholar the power to present things word for word after hearing it just once. Mastery over Samveda adds charm, softness and sweetness to a person's voice. Eloquence in speech is the power gained from digested knowledge. These are all the special facts told by modern experts of Vedas.

Hanuman can win hearts. Rama understood this. That is why Rama understood by listening to some words of Hanuman that if a cruel enemy holding a weapon in his hand hears Hanuman's conversation, he will leave his weapon and bow down before him. According to Tulsidas ji, knowledge refines a man and makes him gentle.

Hanuman is inquisitive. There is a popular story in this regard. Hanuman expressed his desire to acquire knowledge from the best teacher of the universe in his childhood. His father Kesari was impressed by this inquisitiveness in Hanuman's childhood days. A small child is curious to know about the universe. He pointed towards the Sun God. When Hanuman approached the Sun god for admission to the school, the Sun refused to admit him citing lack of space in the classroom.

There were already 60 lakh sages seated on the chariot revolving around the Sun. No one could stop Hanuman. Hanuman explained to his teacher that he didn't actually need a place to sit. He just needed his permission. The Sun looked at the child Hanuman in surprise and then happily granted permission to the enthusiastic student.

According to the story, in those times, like today, research on the Sun was being done by arranging all the disciples in a satellite. For this, the flying school was floating around the orbit of the Earth. Hanuman ji was also in this flying school. Hanuman ji came out of the flying school and started flying in front of his teacher parallel to him. Depending on the direction of the chariot, Hanuman ji had to fly sometimes forward and sometimes backward. Despite facing constant inconveniences, Hanuman ji paid attention to the teachings being given and absorbed every word like a sponge. In only sixty revolutions of the Sun, Hanuman ji assimilated all the Vedas and became proficient in all the supporting sciences of the Vedas.

Along with this, Hanuman ji learned nine grammars in just nine days. He also understood all the rules of grammar.

It was Hanuman ji's thirst for knowledge that he had acquired much before other classmates. Think about it. Is Hanuman not the first person to do research on the Sun? Is Hanuman not the first astronaut? If this is not so, then how did NASA scientists start research in space. Where did he get the idea of sending passengers into space? Where did the curiosity to understand the Sun arise from? All this happened because of Hanuman and today all scientists including NASA are busy garnering accolades on the strength of Hanuman's teachings and knowledge.

This is why Hanuman is considered among the most knowledgeable. He was also the most learned among the great scholars. Hanuman was also the incarnation of all the qualities of knowledge. He was not only the ocean of knowledge but also the ocean of virtues. In *Jai Hanuman Gyan Gun Sagar Jai Kapis Tihu Lok Ujagar*, the word 'Kapi' means vanar or monkey. He was humble. His humility stole the heart of Rama.

There is an interesting incident. It is believed that even before taking incarnation in the form of Rama, Lord Vishnu ordered all the gods to take birth on earth as monkeys. On hearing Vishnu ji's order, Lord Shiva also became very eager to appear as a monkey. Lord Shiva explained to his wife Sati that he was waiting for an opportunity to serve Rama. He imagined taking a form that was less than human form. He found the monkey form most suitable. A human being may hesitate to engage another human being in petty service, but the service of a monkey would be acceptable without hesitation.

Thus Lord Shiva chose the monkey form to make his contribution to the Ram Leela. He wanted to focus on his service and not be distracted by the presence of his wife, so he decided to remain celibate in that role. Sati became sad and disappointed at not being able to assist her husband in this incarnation. Then suddenly an idea came to her mind that would satisfy both of them. She proposed to Lord Shiva that she could incarnate as the tail of a monkey. Shiva agreed and thus Hanuman was born. He was Rudra and Shakti combined together.

Why did Tulsidas ji write the line *Jai Kapis Tihun Lok Ujagar*? An incident in this regard is found in the stories of the Vedic period. Keeping in mind the expansion of the subject, the essence of the story is presented here. As per the legend, Indra discovered two galaxies missing from the universe. He informed Lord Vishnu. Indra and Vishnu went to Brahma to know the reason behind the disappearance of the two galaxies. Brahma told them how the *kamandalu* (an oblong water pot) fell from his hand and the future events were shattered.

Brahma recalled and told, "A demon named Kaalant was also stored inside the ewer. Now he is missing."

Kaalant was to be born at the end of Brahma's life after 33 years. He had the power to eat all the universes including galaxies, planets and stars. He could even swallow the Adityas. Lord Vishnu and Lord Brahma were wondering what to do. Lord Vishnu remembered Hanuman. Hanuman was one person who could surely save the world.

As usual, Lord Vishnu found Hanuman meditating on his lord Lord Rama. As it was an emergency situation, he apprised him of the predicament faced by the universe. The situation was so bad that Kaalant even swallowed the Kaal Chakra. Without wasting even a minute, Hanuman knew what he had to do and he set out in search of Kaalant. All the gods blessed Hanuman and gave him the power to conquer Kaalant. Hanuman first tried to convince him to go back to kamandalu and come when the right time comes. Kaalant flatly refused. He challenged Hanuman to a duel. During the battle, the demons reached Pari Lok. A demon had kidnapped the daughter of the queen.

Hanuman went to the demon to save the girl in distress. The demon told Hanuman about the curse put on him by a female demon. To remove the curse he needed a special pearl from the queen of angels. The luster of the pearl was enough to free him. But the queen refused to give her pearl and the demon was left with no option but to kidnap her daughter. Hanuman found out that the pearl was in safe custody in chal lok. Hanuman also reached there but the planet was captured by the dwarfs. Hanuman fought the dwarfs and returned chal lok to its original king, who happily gave chal lok to Hanuman.

Hanuman dropped the dwarfs at their planets, but being in a hurry, he reached the wrong planet underwater. He also saved the king of that planet, who gave him a compass, a direction indicator. Hanuman would come out of the Kaal Chakra and return to his universe. Coming back, he chased Kaalant. He got into a battle with him. Kaalant being antimatter, Hanuman thought of swallowing him. Diving into his stomach, he found a new strategy to defeat him. He allowed Kaalant galaxies and planets that had disappeared to come back. He also found Arun Dev and requested him to turn the kal chakra in a clockwise direction.

Not surprisingly, everything started falling back to its place. Everyone except Kaalant started having severe stomach pain and made Hanuman vomit. Then Lord Vishnu and Lord Brahma explained to Kaalant that if he kept the Sun God hidden, he would also die prematurely. Everything should happen at its time. Kaalanta had suffered a lot so he understood their reasoning and agreed to go back to Kamandalu. Before that, he freed the Sun God, galaxies, planets and stars and normalcy was restored. Hanuman had saved the world once again and hence *Jaya Kapisa Tihun Lok Ujagar* was proved again.

❐

***Ram Doot Atulit Bal Dhaama |***
***Anjani Putra Pavan Sut Naama || 2***

[You are the messenger of Lord Rama, a storehouse of immense power and known as the 'son of Anjani' and the 'son of Vayu Dev'.]

## The Essence

Since ancient times, there has been a special tradition among writers that they portray the character of their hero or main character in a very dignified manner. From the childhood of the hero till the end of the book, the writer arranges special words to highlight every aspect of the hero. Tulsidas ji is also no exception to this. He has not accepted Hanuman's strength (arm strength, intelligence, cleverness, management etc.) as ordinary but uses the sentence *'Atulit Bal Dhaama'*. Atulit means that which cannot be compared and Dhama means storehouse. Hanuman is not ordinary but extraordinarily strong. This is the real form of Hanuman ji. This statement of Tulsidas ji is also confirmed in Hanuman Chalisa.

In childhood itself, Hanuman's mother Anjana told him a secret which Hanuman remembered all his life. The moment he meets his Guru, he will have an overwhelming experience. Brahma had gifted it to him in his childhood with the condition that it would not be visible to anyone except one. Brahma ji had said that the one who sees this gem will be Hanuman's master. When Rama asked him about that jewel, Brahma ji's statement was confirmed. Rama was his eternal master. Hanuman was Rama's eternal servant.

The moment Hanuman first came in front of Lord Rama, the first sight of his eternal master convinced him that this was his eternal refuge. He was getting overwhelmed. Hanuman was in the disguise of a beggar sanyasi. Rama asked him why a beggar was wearing a diamond necklace around his neck. On hearing this, Hanuman was stunned by that question. It was an invisible necklace. This necklace was worn by Hanuman since his childhood. It was not visible to anyone till date. Rama asked Hanuman to introduce himself. Hanuman replied that he was Sugriva's servant. Rama was hurt to hear that Hanuman was Sugriva's servant. Hurt Rama stepped back allowing hurt Lakshmana to continue the conversation. As soon as Hanuman saw Rama retreating, he knew that he had made a grave mistake in their very first meeting. From now on Rama would scrutinize his every action very closely. He hoped that he would win Rama's trust once again.

Rama met Sugreeva for the first time. Sugreeva welcomed Rama. He requested Rama to sit on the branch of a tree. Sugreeva sat on the same branch with Rama. This meant that he considered himself Rama's equal. Sugreeva did not give Lakshman place to sit. Lakshman stood there. Hanuman felt bad on seeing this. He didn't want to lose any opportunity to win Rama's trust. Hanuman immediately brought a branch of sandalwood tree and gave it to Lakshman and requested him to sit on it.

Hanuman himself sat down on the ground near Lakshman. He showed respect to Lakshman and pacified the insult done by Sugreeva. Hanuman impressed Rama by hitting two targets with one arrow. Rama spent four months of the rainy season in Kishkindha and during this Chaturmas Hanuman succeeded in winning Rama's heart. From being Sugriva's servant, now Hanuman became Rama's messenger. This is the best example of Hanuman's intelligence.

After winning the trust of Rama, Hanuman became Rama's confidant. Sugriva and Hanuman discussed in detail the purpose for which Rama had wandered to reach the Kishkindha region. Hanuman ji assured Rama that he would leave no stone unturned to find mother Sita. Seeing Hanuman's confidence and determination, Rama decided to give his ring to Hanuman. Hanuman became Ramdoot (messenger of Lord Rama) and started searching for Sita.

Who is *Ramdoot Atulit Bal Dhaama*? To prove this, Tulsidas tells in the next line - *Anjani-Putra Pavan Sut Naama*, that is, he is the son of Anjani and Pawan (Vayu God), whom we respectfully call Hanuman. Tulsidas ji indicates the story of Hanuman's birth through this sentence structure.

Kesari and Anjana were invited to visit Badri Narayan by the disciples of the powerful sage Vishwambhar. Along with Hanuman ji, they set out for the Himalayas. After a difficult journey, the monkey family completed the journey to the peaks of Badrinath and appeared before Rishi Vishwambhar. The sage took the whole family to visit Lord Badri Narayan.

On seeing Badri Narayan, the infant Hanuman excitedly raised both his hands and said loudly - 'Rama'. Kesari immediately explained to his son that this is the deity of Badri Narayan. At the same time a harsh voice was heard. The old vow was broken. The impossible had happened. No one present there could believe this. Rishi Vishwambhar was surprised. He had said something other than the name of Lord Narayan for so long. To know the secret of this unexpected incident, all the disciples gathered around their Guru. The Guru told the disciples "He had observed this fast due to the concern to save the saint community from persecution at the hands of demons."

At the beginning of this fast, Lord Brahma had predicted that the name of Rama would be said from the mouth of an innocent child. It would lead to the destruction of demons.

He further said, "Lord Brahma had further prophesied that Lord Rama and Lord Shiva would incarnate as Hanuman to destroy the negative forces."

Then Sage Vishwambhar declared that this child is none other than the abode of Lord Shiva and Shakti. Lord Rama will always reside in his heart and together they will destroy the demonic forces. "True! This is Rama."

❒

***Mahavir Vikram Bajrangi |***
***Kumati Nivaar Sumati Ke Sangi || 3***

*A great warrior, brave and valiant like a thunderbolt, you dispel evil thoughts and are the companion of those with pure hearts.*

## The Essence

Tulsidas ji has told us about Hanuman ji in detail and now in the next quatrain, he gives information about Hanuman ji's courage and valour and says that Hanuman ji is brave and valiant like a thunderbolt.

Vajra is a Sanskrit word which has two meanings — lightning and diamond. Apart from this, vajra also means a weapon won in a war. According to the Puranas, a weapon similar to the tip of a spear is said to be the main weapon of Indra. The story of its origin is written in Brahmin texts and Puranas. It is mentioned in the Rigveda that Indra destroyed the demons with the bone of sage Dadhichi. It is described in Aitareya Brahmana as follows. As long as Dadhichi was alive, the demons would run away on seeing him but when he died, the demons started creating havoc. Indra went to Pushkar in search of Sage Dadhichi.

There he came to know that Dadhichi had passed away. Indra started looking for his bones. He found his skull bone in Pushkar area. Indra killed the demons by making a Vajra from it. It is written in Bhagwat that Indra had made a Vajra from Dadhichi's bone to kill Vritrasura. According to Matsyapurana, when Vishwakarma had mounted the Sun on the Bhramayantra and turned it, the sharp edge that came out of it was used to make Vishnu's Chakra, Rudra's spear and Indra's Vajra.

It is written in Vamanpurana that when Indra had entered Diti's womb, he found a lump of flesh near the child. When Indra pressed it in his hand, it became long and a hundred knots were seen in it. The same became hard and turned into a Vajra. Similarly, there are different stories in other Puranas as well. Its synonyms are: Hladini. Kulish. Shatakoti. Shaba Dambholi, Dambh, etc. Apart from this, Vidyut means lightning. The work of lightning is to fall or flash.

Today scientists have proved that lightning falling from the sky is a discharge of electricity. A single stroke of lightning can heat the air around it up to 30,000° Centigrade (C) or 54,000° Fahrenheit (F). Due to this extreme heat, the air expands explosively. With its expansion, lightning gives a sharp shock which comes in the form of a wave. Along with this, it turns into a loud sound wave which is known as thunder.

One meaning of Vajra is diamond. It is a type of iron. It is very strong. Many types of Vajra iron have been mentioned in the texts of medicine. It is a garland. Vajra is one of the twenty-two Vyatipat Yogas in astrology. Persons born in Vajra Yoga are as strong and powerful as a thunderbolt. Like the vajra, their arms have amazing power and strength. They are proficient in many kinds of knowledge and are adept in using weapons.

They usually do not have to face shortage of money. According to Vastu Vidya, it is a pillar whose middle part is octagonal. It is a symbol of Vishnu's feet. It is also called mica. It is the Kolilaksha tree. It is white kush. It is also kanji. It is vajrapushpa. It is dhatri. It is thuhar tree or sehund. It is a great grandson of Krishna who was the son of Aniruddha. It is the name of a son of Vishwamitra.

It also stands for Chakra symbol in Buddhism. It symbolizes child or infant. It is a posture or position of asana, a type of sitting. Vajra-asana is a sitting posture. Start by sitting back on your heels and keeping your knees, feet and toes together. Keeping the back straight, place the palms of your hands on your thighs. Breathe slowly through your nostrils and sit in this position for at least three minutes. A type of military formation. A tool for piercing gems, precious stones, etc. A weapon as hard as a thunderbolt and deadly. Harsh language. Language is as hard as a thunderbolt. A plant called Aklabeer. As hard as a thunderbolt. Very hard or strong. Extremely firm and robust as if when this spice dries, it will become a thunderbolt. Fierce. Terrible.

There is a couplet by Jayasi: *Vajra Agni Birhini Hiya Jara. Sulagi Sulagi Dahi Kai Bhaai Chhara.* In which there is a bone or a surgery. It is thorny. It is written in Vaman Puran that when Indra had entered Diti's womb, he found a lump of flesh there near the child. When Indra pressed it in his hand, it became long and a hundred knots were visible in it. The same became hard and turned into a thunderbolt. Similarly, there are different stories in other Puranas too. In mythology, the vajra has significance, power and symbolism.

The word "vajra" is derived from Sanskrit and can be translated as "thunderbolt" or "diamond". It represents indestructibility, power and invincibility. The vajra is primarily associated with Lord Indra, the king of gods and the lord of thunder and lightning. The vajra is made of brass or bronze with four prongs on each end that rotate around the middle fifth to form the shape of a lotus bud. The vajra with nine prongs is rarely used. How to make your body strong like a vajra? Exercise. Doing regular physical exercise is the most important way to strengthen your body.

Physical exercise can develop strength, power and durability in you. Try doing a variety of exercises such as weight training, yoga, cardio exercises, and compound exercises. A mythological and ritual tool, symbolizing the qualities of diamond (indestructibility) and vajra (irresistible power). It is described as a divine weapon that has immense power and indestructibility. Vajra is often depicted as a double-headed, diamond-shaped weapon with a handle in the middle.

Vajra symbolizes both the indestructible nature of the diamond and the indomitable power of the thunderbolt. Indra's famous weapon is the Vajra, which can be considered as the synonym of lightning. Indra's thunderbolt was created by a special deity named 'Tvashta'. Vajra is the most powerful weapon possessed by Indra, who is the god of rain, storm and lightning. The powerful god first used his weapon on the demon named Vritra, who symbolizes drought in the Rigveda. Divine powers are those holy powers that inspire any human being to do good deeds. Some get more of these powers and some get less. - These powers support us and also help us.

Vajra was the eldest son of Aniruddha and his second wife Usha. He was the only survivor of the Yadu dynasty after the terrible devastation caused by Gandhari's curse. Vajra was made the king of Indraprastha at the request of Krishna after the Yadava fratricide just before the Pandavas went into exile. The weapon called vajra is used by people like the wrathful god Vajrapani as a mace to suppress any external or internal obstacle and is thus an instrument of compassion and an efficient means to lead to the imperishable state of wisdom. Indra is described as using the vajra to kill sinners and ignorant persons. The Rig Veda states that this weapon was made for Indra by Tvashta, the maker of divine instruments. The related story tells that Indra killed the demon Vritra, who had assumed the form of a serpent, using the vajra held in his hand.

One who shows extraordinary bravery in battle is called a Yudhveer. One who has the courage to forgive others by showing extreme compassion is called a Dayaveer. The courage to give charity makes a person a Daanveer. The courage to stick to the path of Dharma despite great odds makes a person a Dharamveer. And the one who has the courage to renounce attachment is called Tyagveer. Each of these subtypes of valour requires immense courage and resolve. Even one of these types of courage is admired and worshipped by the world.

When Hanuman was in Lanka he single-handedly fought the entire Lankan army. Ravana sent hordes of demons to finish off Hanuman, but none of them returned alive. He sent some of his best men including heroes like Jambumali and his own son Akshay Kumar. But they all ended up in the grave. It takes a lot of courage and confidence to stand alone against an entire army and that too in your own country without any allies. Hanuman was the greatest warrior in history. He fought not for any personal gain but to help others. You will not find a single story of Hanuman where he fought for himself.

Hanuman lived a life of compassion and dedicated himself to serving others despite the hardships. He was a perfect Dayaveer who lived a compassionate life. Even today when we find ourselves hopeless and lost, we turn to Hanuman, knowing very well that his compassion is omnipresent and endless. There are many charitable people in this world. But they give only a sliver of their wealth to charity. But the one who donates himself is the greatest charity. Hanuman completely surrenders himself to those who sincerely touch his heart. Once Hanuman came to the conclusion that Rama was worthy of his devotion, he completely surrendered himself to Lord Rama with his mind, body and words.

Vanar Sena (the monkey army) was discussing who would cross the 800-mile long ocean? Angad claimed, "I can easily cross the ocean and reach Lanka." He said it in excitement but he was not sure whether he would return or not. Angad knew about the deadly attractions and temptations of Lanka. He also knew his limitations and weaknesses in self-control. He doubted whether he would be able to resist the temptations in Lanka and return?

Hanuman not only crossed the 800 mile ocean to reach Lanka but also crossed the ocean of temptations present inside Lanka. He was a true Dharamveer who had the courage to stay on the path of Dharma despite great temptations hidden as obstacles to distract from the higher goals of life.

Hanuman was the most powerful and capable person of his era. He gave up his attachment to fame and followership to remain a lifelong follower of Lord Rama. Hanuman is truly Mahavir. *Mahavir Vikram Bajrangi.*

Hanuman's Annaprashan ceremony was performed. Hanuman first ate some grains. His hunger increased. One day he was turning from side to side with hunger. Sage Narad appeared. He gave him some fruits. But the hunger didn't go away. Finally, Narad Muni pointed towards the sun. Hanuman took a leap thinking the sun to be some big fruit. Frightened by the sight of a baby monkey heading towards the Sun, the planets began to change their orbits to stay out of its path. The planets Venus, Mercury and Jupiter got separated and the sudden change in their positions caused tremendous disturbance on Earth as these planets influence astrological calculations that affect people's lives. When Lord Surya saw the small group of impending disaster, he called out to his friends, Kala, Varuna and Agni for protection.

Kala arrived first. Hanuman was attacked. An intense battle ensued. Kala expanded himself to enormous size and Hanuman immediately expanded himself to equal him. Hanuman then challenged Kala. He said that anyone can expand easily, but only the great can shrink. Hanuman began to shrink himself. Kala fell into the trap of ego and made himself even smaller than Hanuman. Hanuman then came back to his original size and let Kala go only when he pleaded with him and promised not to interfere in his affairs.

Then came Agni's furious attack. Unable to cause any harm, Agni realized that it was none other than Rudra incarnate. He stepped aside and was replaced by Varuna's icy cold missiles. None of them could harm or even disturb Hanuman's progress towards the sun. Kala, Agni and Varuna accepted defeat and left with their heads bowed. Sage Narad smiled from a distance. He was pleased to see the ego of the gods thwarted as they were earlier mocking this monkey incarnation of Rudra. Hanuman was only a few inches away from the Sun. Rahu was approaching the Sun from the other direction. Now two contenders were rushing to swallow the Sun.

The Sun was trapped and scared. Having easily defeated Rahu, Hanuman advanced menacingly towards the Sun. As a last resort, the Sun God tried to warn Hanuman about the grave consequences of coming close to him. When Hanuman ignored his warnings, he increased his anger. The heat became so intense that the entire universe began to sweat. The inhabitants of the earth had no idea why the unbearable heat had suddenly increased. Unable to bear the pangs of hunger, Hanuman grabbed the Sun. The entire world was immersed in darkness.

To punish Hanuman for his mistake and to stop him from snatching the Sun from the sky, Indra, the king of the gods, intervened and struck Hanuman with a thunderbolt. The thunderbolt struck Hanuman's chin and he fell down dead on the earth with his jaw broken.

Indra was stunned to see the audacity of the little monkey whose mouth was swollen with the Sun. In anger, he threw his Vajra weapon straight at Hanuman's face. The thunderbolt struck Hanuman straight and broke his jaw. The blow was so severe that Hanuman was pushed backwards and fell down unconscious. His mouth opened up on his chin involuntarily.

Hanuman was caught by his father and taken to safety in a cave. He was enraged by the unfair attack on his son. He withdrew all the air from the world. The world was in an uproar due to the lack of Prana Vayu. To appease Hanuman's father Vayu, all the gods including Lord Brahma appeared before Vayu and asked for forgiveness for their injured son. He revived the child and gave him infinite blessings which made the child powerful, invincible and truly immortal. Then another boon was given to Hanuman. His body would become as strong as Indra's thunderbolt. With this boon Hanuman got a new name Bajrangi. That means one whose body is as strong as a thunderbolt. He is *Mahavir Vikram Bajrangi*.

Hanuman became Sugreeva's servant without any invitation. Hanuman was appointed by the Sun God to protect Sugreeva. Sugreeva and Bali were both brothers. Bali used to kick his brother's head 12 times every day. Sugreeva lived on a mountain called Rishimukh. Bali could not set foot on it due to a curse. Sage Matang managed to attack him from the air without stepping on the mountain. Bali had to jump across four oceans to reach Rishimukh Mountain. Bali had to kick his helpless brother in the head before moving on to his next destination. Hanuman coming into Sugriva's life changed the equation.

The next time Bali attempted to kick Sugriva's head, Hanuman caught his feet in mid-air. He pulled Bali's feet down in an attempt to make him touch the mountain, thereby making Matang Rishi's curse come into effect instantly and Bali's tyranny ended forever.

Bali pleaded with Hanuman to let him go. He promised that he would never trouble Sugreeva again. Bali learned an unforgettable lesson and Sugreeva was relieved of the pain. He expressed his gratitude to his newly-elected guardian-cum-guide. Thus, from the moment Hanuman entered the Ramayana, he declared to destroy those who support adharma with an evil mind, while he stood with those who harbor positive, uplifting religious thoughts, thus being regarded as the destroyer and companion of evil.

❒

***Kanchan Varan Viraj Subesa |***
***Kaanan Kundal Kunchit Kesha || 4***

[Your body is golden in colour, and you are beautifully dressed. You wear earrings and your hair is curly.]

## The Essence

Hanuman's mother Anjana named him Sundar. The reason behind naming him Sundar was that she wanted her child to be beautiful both internally and externally. The sunlight had an effect on Hanuman's body. His body had a golden aura of the sun. This is why he is known as Kanchana Baran. It is believed that Hanuman's golden colour increased further when he started his journey to the south in search of Mata Sita.

It dispelled the darkness of night and more importantly the darkness of ignorance. Thus Hanuman became the guiding force for the monkey army which was exploring the southern region in search of Sita. This explains his Kanchana Baran golden coloured body.

When Hanuman entered Ravana's palace in Lanka, he searched everything and finally entered the royal bedroom. In a sea of ordinary beds Hanuman saw a huge golden bed inlaid with gorgeous stone with a white canopy in the middle of the room. It had a soft sheepskin and silk sheet and in place of a bedpost four women were waving large silk fans which helped spread the fragrance from the divine incense. Deeply asleep on the bed among the hundreds of women was the powerful Ravana, the ruler of Lanka. The bright light of the golden lamps next to the bed gave his youthful body a golden glow. Ravana was like the moon in the full sky.

Hanuman was amazed to see the unique view of the Ashoka forest of Lanka. Then Hanuman was very happy to find Sita. He started jumping around, leaping, laughing and singing while kissing her tail.

The monkey boy was born with earrings in both his ears. But that was not all. Those earrings were made of the five metals that Bali had fed to his mother. The metal mixture was transformed into beautiful earrings which adorned the child's ears. From then on, child Hanuman was famous for many virtues, but the most special of them was his mystical earrings. *Kanan Kundala Kunchita Kesa.*

With this most deadly liquid weapon in his hand, Vayu went out of his chamber. Calling his most trusted maid, he handed over the liquid to her with instructions to feed it to the pregnant Anjana, who was a Vanara woman and the wife of Kesari, the chief of a section of the Vanara army. The maid went to Anjana's bedroom and with great confidence, offered the poison to the pregnant woman and assured her that it was all for the health and quick growth of the child in her womb. Anjana gratefully accepted the liquid. The maid waited till Anjana had drunk the entire potion. When she saw the woman herself drinking the liquid, she took the empty vessel and left.

❐

***Hatha Vajra Aur Dhwaja Viraje |***
***Kaandhe Moonj Janeu Saaje || 5***

[You hold a mace and a flag in your hands and wear a sacred thread made of munja grass on your shoulder.]

## The Essence

A few years after giving birth to Hanuman, Anjana had to return to her divine abode when the curse period was over. Hanuman wanted to get his mother back. Hanuman left for Swargaloka (heavenly abode) to try and bring his mother back.

Kesari decided to try something on his part too. He went to a powerful sage named Matang Rishi who started a yagna that would take Kesari to heaven through yoga.

Hanuman reached heaven where he met Urvashi. She explained to Hanuman that it was not possible to take his mother back. By then Anjana had regained her original form as Punjakasthali. Hanuman had not heard anything about it, so Urvashi suggested that the only person who could help him was Durvasa Muni who had cursed him in the beginning.

Hanuman immediately set out to meet Durvasa Muni who was held captive in Yakshaloka. This is a long episode. It is not possible to elaborate here due to lack of space.

Hanuman Ji overcame many obstacles and turned the conflict in his favour. Not only were the Gods grateful for the release of Durvasa Muni from the clutches of the Yakshas, the Saptarishis also expressed their gratitude to him. Such was Durvasa Muni's gratitude to Hanuman that he agreed to grant permission to

Punjakasthali. Indra himself decided to accompany Hanuman and his mother on the return journey to Kishkinda on Prithvi Lok (Earth realm).

While the three of them were on their way, they were attacked by a demon named Vidyutsur, who was sent by Ravana. He was one of Ravana's most powerful demons. Indra advised Hanuman to go ahead with his mother while he would take care of that demon. But Hanuman was in no mood to turn away from a good fight. Besides, it was his moral duty to accompany Indra during a crisis. Vidyutsur attacked Indra faster than anticipated and as a result Indra's weapon slipped from his hand. Extremely cautious Hanuman jumped to pick up the Vajra weapon. Vidyutsur turned around and faced Hanuman, who by now had prepared himself for battle while his entire demonic guard was guarding him. Hanuman returned with his monkey form as Anjana. While Indra was busy destroying the demon army, Hanuman leapt high to attack Vidyutsur.

With a swift move of his right hand, Hanuman slit Vidyutsur's throat with the sharp-edged Vajra weapon. In a short while all that was left of the demons was a pile of corpses. Hanuman extended the Vajra to return it to Indra. When Indra extended his hand to take it back, there was a loud celestial announcement that the Vajra now belonged to Hanuman who had saved Swargaloka from the demons and Indra should let him keep it.

Indra happily gifted Hanuman the Vajra weapon along with Vijay Dhwaj and blessed him to always be victorious in every battle in life. Indra also announced that from that day Hanuman would be known as Vajradhari and Dhwajdhari. The literal translation of *Hatha Vajra Aur Dhwaj Biraje* is that Hanuman holds the Vajra and Dhwaj in his hands. Vajra means thunderbolt, a weapon of Lord Indra, and Dhwaj means flag. Vajra and Dhwaj also refer to the lines on Hanuman's hands rather than just the physical objects that he carried. The lines of the Vajra and Dhwaj on his palms symbolize immense power and fame, respectively.

During their exile the Pandavas travelled to many forests. They met many sages. These were times of great sadness, having lost all their wealth and suffered much humiliation. During such depressing times, the Pandava brothers sought wisdom from the sages to help them deal with their pain. The sages narrated various histories about kings in the past who faced the challenges in life with dignity. One such was blessed with longevity. Markandeya Rishi narrated about that time, Arjuna conversed with the great sage Markandeya who told the story of Lord Rama and how he took the help of an army of monkeys to build a bridge over the ocean to rescue his wife.

When helped Arjuna, a doubt bothered him. Though Arjuna didn't ask Markandeya Rishi the story of Rama's struggle and determination, he kept pondering over it. While he was standing on the bank of a lake thinking about his doubts that if Rama was such a powerful archer then why did he need to use an army of monkeys to build a bridge that could easily be built using arrows, an old monkey came and stood next to him. As if furthering Arjuna's thoughts, the monkey said that it would be impossible for a bridge of arrows to withstand the weight of an army of monkeys.

Arjuna disagreed and argued that an expert archer could achieve any target with his arrows. In fact, he boasted that even a small-time archer like him could easily achieve that feat. The old monkey challenged Arjuna to build a bridge of arrows on the lake that could handle his feeble weight. Within a minute, Arjuna built a bridge of arrows. He said that if the bridge collapsed with the monkey's weight then he would sacrifice his life. The monkey didn't even bother to step on it, but instead dropped his tail on it and the bridge collapsed.

The old monkey urged Arjuna to try again with more concentration. Arjuna built a strong bridge and this time it bore the weight of the monkey. But when the monkey reached the middle it collapsed. Disappointed, Arjuna was ready to end his life. Just then, an old Brahmin appeared and stopped him from jumping into the pyre. He told both of them that any conflict between two people requires a neutral witness. The Brahmin agreed to be the witness if they tried once.

Once again Arjuna built a bridge with greater concentration. The monkey walked on it but nothing happened. He jumped on it and still nothing happened. The old monkey discarded his disguise and assumed his true Hanuman form. Stretching himself to a gigantic size he began jumping on the bridge, still nothing happened. Both of them were shocked. How could the bridge bear so much weight? Then they realized that the old Brahmin was none other than their revered Lord Hanuman. Arjuna saw him as Krishna and Hanuman saw him as Rama. On Lord's feet, he promised never to be arrogant. Lord then blessed both His devotees and wished that they both unite for the upcoming war against the Kauravas. He instructed Hanuman to sit on the flag of Arjuna's chariot. Hanuman's presence on Arjuna's flag would announce auspiciousness and serve as a declaration of his imminent victory. Hanuman was the one who held Lord Rama's victory flag in the war against Ravana, so his presence on Arjuna's flag would indicate certain victory.

Hanuman sits on the flag of the chariot of each devotee of the Lord, indicating His victory against the deceptive forces. Thus Hanuman is called *Dhwaj Viraje*, the one who sits on the *Vijay Dhwaj* or the one who holds the victory flag. The practice of placing Hanuman on the war chariot was established by Lord Sri Rama during the war in Treta Yuga, when Indra sent a chariot for Sri Rama. Sri Rama circumambulated the chariot to honor it. Then seated Hanuman with Himself as His own personal assistant. *Haath Vajra Aur Dhwaja Birajay.*

First he was put under the tutelage of Angavahan Rishi. After a short time of learning there, his father Kesari felt that he would do better if he was given more experience and after consulting the wind god, he decided to send Hanuman to learn from the Sun god. While he was under the tutelage of the Sun, Lord Rama was under the tutelage of Sage Vasishta. One day something interesting happened.

Hanuman was learning archery on the Sun planet and Rama was learning archery at Vasishta's ashram on Earth. Hanuman shot an arrow towards the Earth and Rama shot an arrow towards the sky. Both the arrows collided in the air and produced a fierce sound that reverberated throughout the universe. This was his first association with the medium of learning.

After this Hanuman went under the tutelage of Narad Muni to acquire musical skills, Narad Muni taught him singing and playing instruments. Hanuman became so adept at everything that even his teacher was very impressed with him. Once Narada Muni asked him to sing a special song to test his knowledge. Hanuman sang it so sweetly that it melted Narada Muni's heart. Mesmerized by Hanuman, Narada Muni closed his eyes and did not even realize when his *veena* slipped from his hand and fell to the ground. Surprisingly, Hanuman's singing affected not only living beings but also inanimate objects like stones and rocks. The hard stones melted in joy of the song. Narada Muni's *veena* also fell on one of those melted stones.

When Hanuman stopped singing, everything took its original shape and the melted stones regained their hardness. Unfortunately, the *veena* was now stuck in the hard rock. Narada Muni requested Hanuman to sing again to free his *veena*. Hanuman refused to obey and started running here and there.

Helpless Narada Muni ran after the mischievous boy trying to catch him.

After a lot of running, Hanuman returned to the original place and sang. Soon the Veena was released and again came into the hands of Narad Muni. When he asked Hanuman why he had disturbed him, Hanuman gave a very interesting answer. He revealed that he wanted the dust of his Guru's feet to fall everywhere and sanctify it. This was Hanuman's style of doing so.

Janeu represents the knowledge of Vedic scriptures. Wearing a sacred thread worn by Brahmins is a sign of being a student. Hanuman remained an eternal student, always absorbed in listening and learning from many teachers. Thus a sacred thread always remains on his shoulders, which proclaims his eternal role as a student who is always eager to learn. *Kadhe Munj Janeu Sajai.* The sacred thread on Hanuman's shoulder also signifies that Hanuman was well versed in the scriptures, as he was sacred.

The thread ceremony initiates a person into the formal study of Vedic literature. Once Rama himself explained the secret of Brahmavidya to Hanuman. The Sri Rama Rahasya Upanishad states that great sages and saints like Sanaka, Sanandana, Sanatana and Sanat Kumara learned the hidden secrets of Rama Tatva from Hanuman. Other sages like Prahlad were his disciples. The thread in the *Janeu Saaje* is described as the ornament of Hanuman which was the treasure of his knowledge.

❐

***Sankar Suvan Kesri Nandan |***
***Tej Prataap Maha Jag Vandan || 6***

[You are the incarnation of Lord Shiva and the son of Kesari. Your glory and valour are revered in the entire universe.]

## The Essence

Hanuman ji's character is described in many forms in many Puranas. Hanuman Ji is described as Shankar Suvan, Pavantanay, Kesarinandan, Anjaneya and Shankar himself. Hanuman Ji's various names are related to mysterious incidents. Hanuman's birth story is divine and mysterious.

Rudravatar Shri Hanuman. It is mentioned in ancient texts that once Lord Shankar was sitting on Mount Kailash with Bhagwati Sati. Incidentally, Lord Shankar said to Sati, "Dear! The one whose name I keep on reciting, he is coming to the world in the form of my Lord. All the gods want to get the opportunity to serve him by getting incarnated with him. Then why should I be deprived of it? I should also go there and fulfill my desire of ages by serving him."

On hearing this from Lord Shiva, Sati thought and said- "Prabhu! This time God is incarnated to kill Ravana. He is your exclusive devotee. He has even cut off his head and offered them to you. In such a situation, how can you help in killing him?" On hearing this, Lord Shiva started laughing. Laughing, he said- "Devi! Just as Ravana has worshipped me, he has also ignored one of my parts. You know that I live in eleven forms. When he worshiped me by offering his ten heads, he left one of my parts without worshipping. Now I can fight against him with that part and serve my Lord. I have decided to take incarnation from the womb of Anjana through the wind god." On hearing this, Bhagwati Sati was very pleased.

In another story, it is described- Lord Vishnu started thinking about the semen of Lord Shambhu that was ejaculated after seeing the form of Mohini, what should be the use of this semen produced by Shambhu? After thinking for a while, both of them (Vishnu and Shambhu) assumed the form of sages and carrying the semen in a leaf-drone proceeded through the forest. After going some distance, they saw a girl who was engaged in severe penance. They went to her and said, "Ascetic girl! What are you doing? Without taking initiation, your penance cannot be successful. So, take initiation from a capable sage soon." After listening to the talk of those two sages, the ascetic girl Anjana thought in her mind, "They are the seers of all times. They are saying that my past is true. So, why not take initiative from them." Thinking this, Anjana said, "Great Sage, you are capable and competent. Where else will I wander to get initiated? You please give me the initiation of mantras."

Then Vishnu, who was in the guise of a sage, gave the initiation of mantras to Anjana. While giving the initiation, he invoked the semen of Lord Shiva with mantras and put it in the womb of Anjana through his ear. Hanuman Ji, born from that semen of Lord Shiva, was known as Anjani Nandan Shankar Suvan. 'Pavantanaya' Shri Hanuman: there was a very beautiful Apsara named Punjikasthala who was famous among the Apsaras.

She was born on earth as a monkey in the form of a lustful monkey due to the curse of a sage. She became famous by the name of 'Anjana' after becoming the wife of the great monkey Kesari. Kesari ruled the mountain Sumeru. Anjana was his beloved wife. One day, the monkey king Kesari and Anjana both were roaming on the mountain peak in the guise of humans. Seeing the beautiful form of Anjana, the wind god was fascinated and he embraced her. Sadhu Charitra Anjana was surprised and said, "Which evil soul is ready to destroy my fidelity towards my husband? I will curse him and reduce him to ashes."

On hearing this from Sati-Sadhvi Anjana, Pawan Dev said, "Sushroni! I have not broken your marital fidelity. If you have any doubts, then clear them. I have made a mental contact. You will have a son from him, who will be equal to me in strength and valour. He will be a servant of God and will be incomparable in strength and intelligence. I will protect him." Thus, Lord Shankar, taking the medium of air in part, produced a son from Anjana's womb. He was later known as Shankar Suvan, Pavanputra, Kesari Nandan, Anjaneya, etc. That same Shri Hanuman became an inseparable part of Lord Shri Ram through his unique service.

Another story is found. Anjana was meditating in a cave in the mountains. While she was engrossed in meditation, someone else was meditating on her beauty. A demon named Shambasadhana, driven by lust, had been keeping an eye on her for the past few days. When he came near her, Anjana panicked and ran away to escape from his clutches. She somehow reached a village of powerful sages. When she told them her trouble of being chased by a demon, the sages replied that the only person who could protect her was the monkey chief Kesari. And what a coincidence! As soon as they told his name, Kesari came. Soon Shambasadhana and Kesari had a meeting.

A fierce battle ensued between the two. Both were so powerful and skilled that none was able to gain the upper hand. Then Shambasadhana began to change form. He assumed the form of a giant elephant and attacked Kesari. Kesari in turn reduced his size dramatically and continued to attack. He sat on the head of the giant elephant and began to strike its head with his fists. Shambasadhana was bleeding profusely but there was no sign of him getting tired or slowing down.

As Kesari began to worry, Anjana prayed for divine help which came in the form of a dream—the only way to kill the demon was to use his own blood. He was immune to everything else. She dipped an arrow in the demon's blood that had spilled all over. Holding the arrow in one hand, with the other she held the bow, moved towards Kesari and threw both in his direction. Kesari, understanding her intention, moved forward and caught both in mid-air. He turned around, re-attached the arrow to the bow and shot it in a single motion. As soon as Kesari landed on the ground, the arrow went ahead and penetrated the demon's body, killing him instantly.

The sages who witnessed this heroic act praised Kesari and Anjana and blessed them profusely. They declared that God had willed them to come together. In fact, he had prophesied that the child born of this marriage would be an incarnation of Lord Shiva himself and would cause the destruction of demonic forces. Thus, with the blessings of the great sages, Kesari and Anjana happily entered into wedlock.

Despite so many prophecies and blessings, the monkey couple could not have any children. They decided to go to Matang Rishi and seek his blessings. It was a long and arduous journey through forests and mountains, which they undertook barefoot. Anjana also vowed to cover this entire journey without any halt. Kesari tried to stop her but seeing her determination he gave up and decided to do his best to help her. As they started walking, thorns and pebbles greeted their path and soon their feet began to hurt with blisters, wounds and cuts. Nonetheless, their resolve was so strong that they kept walking.

Ravana's spies gave him a full report of the sages' prophecy and the worrying baby that was to be born and predicted to cause trouble for him in the future. He decided to nip the problem in the bud before it could brew by sending *Mayavi* (elusive) demoness to stop the monkey couple from completing their journey. Demoness came in the form of a dangerous looking buffalo and blocked their path.

Anjana was not at all worried about the balloon demoness. She kept walking, much to Kesari's shock, crashing straight into the powerful demon ahead. He moved forward and managed to get the demoness out of his way just in time. From this first-hand experience with Kesari, demoness realised that there was no chance of winning against this mighty monkey and he fled to save his life.

Finally, the exhausted couple managed to reach Matang Rishi's ashram. Anjana's legs were completely wounded and bleeding. As she sat to look at them, a cute little baby came running and caressed her wounds very gently. The baby was so beautiful that Anjana was mesmerised. Even Matang Rishi was amazed. He had not seen such a beautiful child anywhere around the ashram. When he looked carefully he realised that the baby was none other than Lord Shiva himself who had come to serve his future mother. After serving Anjana for some time, the baby disappeared.

After returning to Kailash, Lord Shiva shared his blissful experience of serving his mother with Parvati. Back at the ashram, Matang Rishi gave his blessings to Anjana and also gave her the Shiva Mantra. When they started chanting Shiva Mantra, Vayu got the signal that it was time to accumulate the energy of Lord Shiva. Vayu reached Anjana by taking the Shiva energy from the Saptarishis and placed that power in her womb. From that moment onwards, Anjana became as radiant as the Sun. Kesari understood that a divine child was born in his womb.

When Ravana heard this news, he panicked and immediately went to his friend Bali and warned him about the danger coming from Anjana's womb. Initially, Bali did not consider the child growing in Anjana's womb as a threat. But when Ravana reminded him about Kesari's mighty exploits, Bali feared that Kesari's child could surpass him in battle and strength. Kesari was almost impossible to control. And if his son was born more powerful, then surely Vali was very likely to lose his throne. On Ravana's persuasion and provocation, Bali agreed to find a way out. To help Bali, Ravana handed him a mystical arrow. An arrow that can be aimed at even the tiniest of targets and will never miss its mark.

Bali then invited Anjana and Kesari to his palace on the pretext of the festive celebrations of his coronation as the king of Kishkindha. They could not refuse the invitation and joined the celebrations. Bali was a perfect host and with his gracious hospitality he made them feel comfortable in the palace guest house. At midnight when the whole of Kishkindha was asleep, Bali released the mystic. The arrow hit the sleeping Anjana's foetus. The arrow passed through the corridors of the palace, entered the room of the sleeping Anjana and penetrated her womb, destroying the child in her womb.

In extreme pain and agony Anjana cried for help. Kesari rushed to his wife and realised that a mystical weapon had attacked his wife and was destroying the foetus. Nothing was visible externally. But he knew about the existence of such mystical weapons which worked on the power of mantras and did not miss their target.

Feeling immense pain and helplessness, Anjana began chanting the Shiva mantra. As soon as she started, Lord Shiva appeared and neutralized the effect of the arrow. He then revived the child and blessed him to be safe from all types of attacks by external forces. They felt a wave of relief that their child had survived, though they were shaken by the entire incident.

That night, Kesari and Anjana escaped from the palace to reach the safety of their territory. The child they bore turned out to be an incarnation of Shiva himself, often referred to as Shankar. Being the son of Kesari, he is also called Kesari Nandan. Additionally, as the son of the wind god, he is known as Pawan Suta. However, more importantly, he is the favourite child of Lord Rama and is affectionately known as Rama Dulaare. How can one person be a child of so many divine figures? Hanuman is associated with all these personalities on different levels.

Kesari's rule over Sumeru, along with his greatness and indirect parentage, points toward deeper spiritual significance. The golden-shining Sumeru Mountain is considered the land of the gods, with Brahmalok at its centre, surrounded by the realms of other deities. Only the Supreme God, the God of gods, can rule over the world of gods, rather than an ordinary Vanaradhipatika. The name Kesari means "*Ke-Brahmani Saransheelah*," which signifies one who is always surrendered in the form of 'K', Anand-Brahm. This means that the individual who moves and creates is referred to as 'Kesari'. Thus, Kesari embodies the blissful power of Brahma, who governs and controls the realm of the gods. The joy of Brahma serves as the foundation of creation.

According to the Taittiriya Upanishad, all beings are born from Ananda. They live in it and finally get absorbed in it. In the Yaksha Katha of Kenopanishad, it has become clear that Brahma's thunderbolt is constantly raised and due to the fear of him, all the gods like Agni, Surya, Kala, etc. are constantly active. 'Brahma' is Mahakapi. The word 'Kapi' is made from the verb root 'Kap' which means to move. Brahma being omnipresent has reached everywhere and is running the entire universe. Hence he is 'Mahakapi'.

A person exists at three levels, spiritual, life, breath. And the physical body. At the deepest level of the soul. Hanuman was a part of Lord Shiva. His physical body was born from the womb of Anjana through Kesari, thus he is physically the son of Kesari. But since Shiva's energy was transmitted through air, the prana vayu flowing through his body is a contribution of pavana and thus he is a pavana suta. Shankar himself is Kesari Nandan. When Lord Rama conquered Ravana and appointed Vibhishan as the king of Lanka, he requested Hanuman to share this good news with Mata Sita who was held captive in Ashok Vatika. Hanuman immediately reached Ashok Vatika to share the good news. Sita was thrilled to see him again after a month.

In great detail, Hanuman shared the events of the war with Mata Sita and concluded his narration by revealing the news of Ravana's death, Rama's victory and the installation of Vibhishan as the king of Lanka. Sita was very pleased. With this news, eleven torturous months came to an end. She was so pleased with Hanuman that she wanted to give him a fitting reward. But alas, she had nothing at that time. The only thing she could give him was her heartfelt blessings. There was nothing in the three worlds that could match the news that Hanuman had just given her.

Overcome with gratitude and joy, Sita blessed Hanuman that the day he had given her the news would become more special than all other days of the week. He would forever be glorified and worshipped throughout the universe on this day. She blessed Hanuman that all virtues would reside in his heart and Lord Rama would always shower his kindness on him.

Hanuman became famous in the three worlds with the blessings of Mother Sita and the grace of Lord Rama.

By using his talent, strength, and skill and by displaying exemplary attitude in right consciousness, Hanuman forever established a kingdom in the hearts of Sita and Rama and ruled there forever. Sitting on this elevated throne as the King of their hearts, he rules the hearts of the Lord's devotees spread across the three worlds.

His radiance is instantly recognized and admired by all who come in contact with him. Hanuman Ji's brilliance and strength are worshipped by the whole world with the grace of Mother Sita. *Tej Pratap Maha Jaga Bandana.*

❐

***Vidyavaan Guni Ati Chaatur |***
***Ram Kaaj Karibe Ko Aatur || 7***

[You are full of knowledge, virtue and wisdom. You are always ready to carry out the tasks of Lord Rama.]

## The Essence

Tulsidas describes him as composed of pure intellect and foremost among wise men. In *Shri Ram Raksha Stotra*, he is described as the wisest of the wise.

Hanuman is said to be sharp-witted. He was able to learn the entire Vedas in a fortnight. The Sun God was reluctant at the thought of his favourite disciple leaving. So he repeatedly asked Hanuman to forget what he had learnt so that the lessons would stretch for months. He was so pleased with his simplicity and devotion that he let him go and gave him a boon that henceforth whoever takes the name of Hanuman would never forget his lessons! *Vidyavana Guni Ati Chatura.* Yamaraja hurried to Rama's camp to give him a news that really shook him.

He had organized the recitation of Ravana's evil mind and devised a way to defeat Rama by reciting the Chandi Stotra, the completion of which would grant him an iron-club. This will provide an immunity from any defeat. This news spread panic in the monkey army. The mere mention of the Chandi Stotra made them sense impending doom. Rama held a meeting with Vibhishana and other advisors and decided his strategy. After much deliberation, Rama summoned Hanuman and pronounced his final verdict- “I give you complete freedom to go to Lanka and do whatever is necessary to prevent this ritual from being completed. Use any tactics you like, just stop it.”

Hanuman got excited. Hanuman’s main aim was to stop Ravana’s plans.

He entered Ravana’s palace taking the form of a fly. He found out where the ceremony was taking place. Brihaspati, the Guru of the Gods was the chief priest. The guards were pointing their spear at Brihaspati. Brihaspati was helping Ravana only under pressure. Hanuman was ready. He quickly went to Brihaspati and started deleting important words and lines so that Brihaspati would skip the important lines. But he got scared, Brihaspati was hardly referring to the texts because he was reading from memory.

Hanuman started working on another plan. He transformed into a huge dastardly looking demon. Brihaspati’s eyes fell on him, he screamed. He left everything and ran to save his life. Before the guards could see his monstrous form, Hanuman instantly transformed into the size of a fly. Brihaspati was screaming like crazy. There was no way to continue the ritual. Ravana was not one to give up. He decided to start another fire yagna to please Goddess Chandi. He assembled his best Brahmins and in no time began the ceremony. He was running short of Brahmins, yet he had to manage. Soon a young Brahmin came seeking help. The old Brahmin was very happy to have more help. The young Brahmin was enthusiastic and energetic. He helped them sincerely and without any fault.

The delighted Brahmins offered him a boon, to which the Brahmin replied that the best boon was to receive more service. The Brahmins were now completely impressed by his dedication and insisted on fulfilling his wish. Hesitantly, the young man asked him to change two letters in the hymn.

He should pronounce 'Ka' in place of 'Ha'. He assured him that this small change would greatly benefit his lord Ravana; the young man hoped that he was not learned enough to know what this change meant. Only a great Vedic scholar would understand its significance. Fortunately, the Brahmin immediately agreed, seeing nothing wrong in the substitution.

***Jaya tvam devi chamunde, jaya bhutartha karini***

He said 'karini' instead of 'harini'. He knew a little about the destructive effects of the transformation. Instead of being pleased the goddess became absolutely furious. She burned everything around with her fiery eyes. How dare they provoke her anger! She will show them how angry she can be. The sacrifice was a complete failure producing the opposite of the expected results. The Brahmins fled from there.

To save his life, the young man returned to his original form, Hanuman, smiling. He was happy that he knew the significance of the Sanskrit shlokas and could make precise changes in the letters to trick the learned Brahmins. *Vidyavana guni ati chatura*. Mission accomplished, he flew back to his camp.

Hanuman used his knowledge in the most practical way according to the time, place and situation. He was extremely clever and flexible in the use of knowledge keeping in mind the essence and the goal. The result was that he always managed to achieve what he wanted to achieve and that too in the most unique ways.

Inquisitiveness makes the best management. *Ram kaaj* means working for the pleasure of Rama. This is called *seva* or the spirit of service. Hanuman was always eager to serve Rama. *Ram kaaj karibe ko atur.* He dedicated his life in the service of Lord Rama and He got entire satisfaction in doing this. It shows how one can become a dedicated devotee of his guru.

The only person whom Rama did not ask to return was Hanuman. He did not ask Hanuman to leave and Hanuman did not need permission to stay. There was an unspoken agreement and pact between the two. It was an agreement of the heart. Hanuman had no existence without Rama and Rama could not live without seeing Hanuman constantly. Hanuman's greatest satisfaction was to devotedly serve Rama in every possible way.

❒

***Prabhu Charitra Sunibe Ko Rasiya |***
***Ram Lakhan Sita Man Basiya || 8***

[You are fond of hearing of the glorious deeds of Lord Rama. Rama, Lakshmana and Sita dwell in you.]

## The Essence

Before the monkey army set off in search of Sita, Rama met each of them. The soldiers lined up to meet Rama one by one. There was an atmosphere of excitement. The monkeys kept peeping forward to see the heartwarming exchange between Rama and their own kinsmen. Patting them. Encouraging them. Thanking them was very touching.

Hanuman was in front of Rama. Rama decided to test him. He first asked him where he disappeared after doing all this. Hanuman, instead of answering that question, immediately fell at Rama's feet and held him tightly. Rama tried to lift him by holding his shoulders, but Hanuman held his legs tightly. Rama was surprised at this strange behaviour, then Hanuman said- "My dear Lord! Let me always remain in this position. As long as my hands are at your feet. Your hands will remain on my shoulders. As long as I remain in your refuge. You will keep empowering me. The moment I leave your feet, you will leave my shoulders. Your touch and blessings are the source of my strength and abilities. I have been waiting to serve my eternal Guru all my life."

Rama said- "You are talking about blessings. But you have come so late, right at the end. I have no blessings left to give you. All my blessings have been exhausted so what can I give you now?"

Hanuman immediately replied "You may have donated the biggest things you had. O Lord! Surely you still have a small but powerful blessing. To some people you may have given it. To some people you may have given knowledge of scriptures as blessings. You may have given others knowledge or guidance or power or fame or even wealth. I am not looking at such big things as blessings, I am only interested in the smallest thing you have as a blessing and I will be really happy."

Rama got completely confused. Rama wanted to test Hanuman. The tables had turned. Now Hanuman was testing Rama.

Rama asked Hanuman- "What is the smallest thing I have?"

Hanuman said with a smile- "My dear Lord! When you met Lord Parashurama, you told him that the smallest thing you had was Rama. I want you to please give me your name as a gift and blessing. It is very small. But that small word contains the power of the whole universe."

Rama was very impressed. Hanuman's devotion and his wisdom were very special. He succeeded in making a deep impact on the heart of the Lord. Lord Rama embraced Hanuman. At that very moment Hanuman had the name of Rama. He didn't miss any opportunity to chant the name of Rama with great fervor and listen to the Ram Katha. That is, by always listening to the Lord's character, the mind of a human becomes passionate.

Hanuman is virtuous, diligent, sharp-witted, powerful and devoted. When Rama became the king of Ayodhya, mother Sita invited guests for lunch. When everyone had gathered for lunch, Lord Shiva noticed that Hanuman was missing. He asked Rama for his address. Smiling, Rama asked him to check in the gardens. Lord Shiva's curiosity to see Hanuman was much more than his desire to eat food. He and Parvati went out to the garden to find Hanuman. There they heard a very unique sound which sounded like someone snoring.

He walked towards the source of the sound. Shiva was surprised to see that it was Hanuman who was sleeping peacefully and snoring under the mango tree, oblivious to the world. What surprised him the most was the sound of snoring! The holy name of Rama came out of the snoring. Rama's name was so deeply embedded in Hanuman's mind and consciousness that even his snoring was making the sound of Rama.

When Shiva's eyes were fixed on Hanuman, Parvati pointed to the tree under which Hanuman was resting. Something magical was happening there. Every leaf of that tree was moving in rhythm with the vibrations of Rama's holy name. Lord Shiva saw this as the most divine Sankirtan of the holy names of his beloved Lord Rama. In immense joy he himself started dancing and chanting Rama's name. Seeing her husband enter into ecstatic trance, Parvati too joined in the singing and dancing. With the divine couple dancing ecstatically and chanting Rama's name, the Gandharvas, Kinnars and Apsaras of heaven also joined in, filling the atmosphere with divine music and singing.

Sita was worried that her guests had not returned from the garden to the palace. She sent Lakshman to call them back. Lakshman hurried to the garden. The atmosphere in the garden was so festive and devotional that Lakshman could not stop himself from participating in the dancing and singing of the holy names. When Lakshman didn't return, Sita first sent Bharat and then Shatrughna, but neither of them returned with the guests. They had all joined the Kirtan festival. Desperate, Sita herself set out to look for them with Rama. When she walked into the garden, she was completely mesmerized by the sight of the dancing and singing festival in full swing. Amidst all this commotion, Hanuman was blissfully sleeping under the mango tree and his sweet snores echoed Rama's name.

Approaching Hanuman, Rama gently sat beside him and touched his head with great affection. Hanuman woke up. Lord Shiva, who was so moved by Hanuman's devotion, glorified him infinitely. Hanuman blushed with shame at being glorified in front of his Guru. Sensing his uneasiness, Sita invited everyone for lunch. Everyone sat down, Sita began serving lunch. She noticed that, as usual, Hanuman had not sat down but had engaged himself in some service. Today she forced him to sit with the guests. Initially, Hanuman was embarrassed to sit with Rama for lunch. He always preferred to eat Rama's leftovers.

But once he started eating he got so excited that he gulped down the huge amount of food. Nothing was satisfying him. No matter how much Sita served, he kept eating more. He kept looking for more and more food. Everyone was amazed to see Hanuman's hunger. Then Sita realized how she could satisfy Hanuman's insatiable hunger. She placed a Tulsi leaf on which was written the name of Rama. As soon as Hanuman ate the leaf, his hunger miraculously disappeared. Lord Shiva and Parvati were very surprised and pleased by Hanuman's devotion. They blessed him that his devotion to Rama would be glorified for centuries, that the devotees of Lord Rama would know him as Sankat Mochan or the destroyer of troubles and that his love for the holy names of Rama and the pastimes of Rama would grow unlimitedly.

After the coronation ceremony of Sita and Rama, all the great personalities who had sacrificed for Rama were called upon. Each was given precious gifts as a token. Hanuman's turn came. Both Sita and Rama were not sure what gift to give. Hanuman's name was called. Rama narrated Hanuman's deeds in detail to everyone. The citizens of Ayodhya were moved to hear Hanuman's service. Sita took out a beautiful diamond necklace from her neck as a gift and gave it to Hanuman. Silence fell in the hall.

Hanuman took it from Sita's hand. Hanuman rotated the necklace and looked at it from all directions. He felt something was missing. Hanuman rotated the necklace again to be reassured. Perhaps Hanuman ji did not see what he was expecting. Then Hanuman caught the big diamond hanging in the middle of the necklace and broke it. Hanuman had destroyed Sita's gift. He kept it in his mouth and broke it into two pieces with his teeth. He observed both the parts. After this Hanuman started breaking the stone of that necklace. He looked carefully. He was disappointed. Finally Hanuman threw the whole necklace on the floor.

This monkey's behavior spread anger among the citizens of Ayodhya. Many voices and questions arose. Insult of Sita's gift in the full auditorium? In response to all the questions Hanuman said only this much, "I was looking for Rama and Sita in the gems. They were not found in any stone inside or outside, so I threw it away."

One person said, "Hanuman should first look in his heart whether Rama and Sita are present in his heart or not."

The next moment blood was scattered everywhere. Hanuman stood in the middle of the hall with his chest torn open, revealing his heart. In his chest was a radiant and beautiful image of Sita and Rama. Not only did they reside in his heart but they also resided in his heart. That is why Tulsidas wrote- *Rama Lakhan Sita Man Basiya.*

Hanuman teaches us to establish the presence of God in our hearts. If we start listening to the praise of God, He can enter through our ears.

❐

***Sukshma Roop Dhari Siyahi Dikhava |***
***Vikat Roop Dhari Lank Jarava || 9***

[You assumed a small form to appear before Sita and a terrifying form to burn Lanka.]

## The Essence

Hanuman was an expert in assuming small and big forms. We all know that while going to Lanka, Hanuman assumed a tiny form seven times as per the need. He contacted Sita in a small form only.

Ashok Vatika was Ravana's favorite garden. Ravana thought it appropriate to keep Sita in a garden with beautiful flowers. Hanuman assumed a very small form and jumped into this garden. He started roaming here and there in the garden. Ashok Vatika was like a dense forest. There were hundreds of types of trees. It was difficult to see any small figure in this dense forest. Hanuman was getting the benefit of this. Using his intelligence, he assumed a small form so that he would not come in the sight of the seven hundred demons deployed for Sita's security and could complete his work easily. Apart from this, Hanuman ji had a heartfelt desire that Sita should address him as son because Rama had become Hanuman's spiritual father, so Sita became his mother in this regard.

The central part of Ashok Vatika was very charming and beautiful. There was a huge tree in the middle of it. A high platform was made under this huge tree. A very beautiful woman in simple attire was sitting on this platform. Hanuman's conscience was awakened. A thought came to his mind that this might be Mother Sita. In excitement, he was eager to jump down from the tree but the very next moment he gave up the idea of jumping. Why? An army of demonesses was strolling below. After some time, Ravana entered the garden with great pomp and show along with the women of his group, carrying various gifts. Ravana had come to meet Sita. Sita once again insulted him. Ravana could not tolerate this insult. He tried to attack Sita but his wife Mandodri came forward. He angrily warned and left from there.

A demoness named Trijata told her companions about her nightmare and said - "In the dream, I saw a monkey destroying Lanka. The whole city is engulfed in flames." Hearing this, the demonesses got scared. In despair, they left Sita alone.

Taking advantage of the opportunity, Hanuman narrated the Rama Katha. Hanuman saw that his story had an impact on Sita. He immediately jumped before Sita. When Sita saw such a cute little monkey, her maternal affection emerged. Sita called him son. Hanuman was pleased with that address and started smiling. Hanuman was before Sita in diminutive form. In the words of Tulsidas ji- *Sukshma Rupa Dhari Siyahi Dikhava.*

Now Hanuman appeared before Sita in a gigantic form. Sita got confused. She asked Hanuman the secret of changing the shape in this way.

Hanuman politely replied that he is basically in the service of Lord Rama. He could take any shape and any responsibility. Sita was very happy to hear the answer.

After this Hanuman ji started creating havoc in Ashok Vatika. In the morning the demonesses woke up. They were surprised to see Ashok Vatika in ruins. When the demonesses saw a monkey, they got scared. Trijata's dream had finally come true. The soldiers moved towards the garden. What had happened in the garden? Their purpose was to find out. Seeing a monkey, the soldiers started running here and there to catch him. The soldiers kept coming and Hanuman kept on destroying Ashok Vatika completely. Many soldiers were killed. Ravana's son Akshay Kumar was also killed.

Hanuman had a boon that no weapon would work on him and Brahma himself had exempted him from Brahma Paash. Ravana did not know this.

Ravana ordered his soldiers to catch the arrogant monkey alive. He sent Indrajit. Indrajit soon succeeded in tying Hanuman with Brahma Pash. Hanuman was tied intentionally. Hanuman wanted to warn Ravana. Ravana wanted to kill the mischievous monkey in the royal court. Vibhishan advised Ravana that this is Rama's messenger. Do not kill the messenger. Then Ravana said- Monkeys are very fond of their tails. Set fire to this monkey's tail. Mysteriously, Hanuman's tail kept growing. As soon as the tail caught fire, Hanuman freed himself from those ropes and jumped out of the royal court. In no time, the golden Lanka burned to ashes. That is, *Vikat Rupa Dhari Lank Jarava*.

❒

***Bhim Roop Dhari Asura Sanhare |***
***Ramachandra Ke Kaja Sanvare || 10***

[You assumed a huge form to destroy demons and completed the work of Lord Rama.]

## The Essence

Everyone knows about Bhima of Mahabharata. Tulsidas ji has mentioned Bhima to explain the power of Hanuman ji. Like Bhima, Hanuman defeated the demons and helped in the work of Ramchandra.

Hanuman ji also showed his incredible courage during the Mahabharata period. It is mentioned that Bhima was amazed by the power of an ordinary looking monkey. He realized that it must be some divine being. With folded hands, he requested him to tell who he really is. The old monkey smiled. Then Hanuman ji assumed his real form and introduced himself to Bhima as the powerful servant and messenger of Lord Rama. Bhima was pleased and embraced Hanuman.

Hanuman promised to help Bhima in the upcoming war with the Pandavas. He taught Bhima the art of mace fighting and wrestling. He also promised him that during the war, he would be present on Arjuna's flag and increase the intensity of Bhima's war cry by adding his voice. Thus, even before the enemy came near, his would be frightened by Bhima's fierce war cry. Probably this is why Tulsidas ji said *Bhima Rup Dhari Asura Sahare*.

Hanuman's entire life was a life of sacrifice. His life was a life of service. The primary and only goal of Hanuman's life was to serve Rama and his devotees to the best of his ability.

Every mission of Rama was accomplished by Hanuman in a very amazing manner. That is why,

It was Hanuman who personally spoke to both Sugreeva and Rama and convinced them to cooperate to achieve their goals and solve each other's problems. Knowing that Sugreeva's monkey mind is unpredictable and can change anytime, he sealed their friendship by making them take an oath of friendship and devotion in a fire sacrifice. He inspired Sugreeva to assemble the entire monkey army. Hanuman ensured that the huge monkey army arrived on time.

Hanuman also played a vital role in building a stone bridge, 80 miles wide and 800 miles long, in just five days. He brought huge boulders, rocks and even mountains from far off places to ensure that the engineers never ran out of supplies of stones to build the bridge. Many times during the war when invincible mystical weapons were used, Hanuman saved everyone's lives, including Rama and Lakshman.

Hanuman was everything for Rama. He was a messenger, a minister, a friend, a servant, an advisor, a writer, a commander and even acted as a vehicle for Rama when needed. Whatever Hanuman did, he did with utmost devotion, risking his life. He never made any excuses and fulfilled commitments, no matter the cost. Food and sleep had no importance for him until his mission was accomplished.

For him, Lord Rama's mission was always paramount. He was the best of the Brahmins. When required, he became the best Kshatriya in wielding weapons in battle. He was the best Vaishy because a Vaishy gives loans and puts the person under his debt; he puts Rama himself under his debt. The dharma of a Shudra is service, who could follow it better than Hanuman? He fulfilled every mission of Lord Rama as an exemplary Brahmin, Kshatriya, Vaishya and Shudra i.e. in every Varna.

❐

***Laye Sanjivan Lakhan Jiyaye |***
***Shri Raghuvira Harashi udd laye || 11***

[You brought the Sanjivani herb and revived Lakshman, for which Lord Rama embraced you in joy.]

## The Essence

Indrajit had entered the battlefield. He was powerful. He was a skilled warrior. He was clever and well versed in war skills. Indrajit operated in invisible mode. He had the mysterious ability to keep himself hidden for a long time.

Fighting Indrajit was not as easy as fighting all the other demons of Ravana's army. The ease with which he shot arrows made the monkeys realize that they had no chance. One of Indrajit's arrows hit Lakshman's chest. This arrow was given to him by none other than Lord Brahma. The divine arrow rendered Lakshman unconscious. There was a huge commotion in the monkey army on seeing its soldiers fall, causing them to panic.

As soon as Lakshman fell, the monkey army started scattering in different directions. Some save their lives, some lose hope. Taking advantage of this, Indrajit struck fiercely. He killed thousands of confused monkeys. Meanwhile, Jambavan reached the scene. He had received information about the fall of Lakshman. As soon as he saw the fallen hero, his first question was, "Is Hanuman alive?"

Jambavan had so much faith in Hanuman's abilities that Hanuman arrived at the scene. Jambavan took Hanuman aside and shared a plan of action with him. He told him the names of four herbs that were available only in the Himalayan Mountains. Jamwant told the name of each herb and its medicinal properties. The first was *Mrita-Sanjeevani*, who could revive a dead person. The second was *Sailya-Karani*, which could remove embedded weapons and heal wounds instantly. The third was *Suvarna-Karani*, which restored the color of the body to its original texture and Samdhani, which could join broken bones and severed limbs.

Hanuman had to bring the herbs before sunrise the next day or else there would be no sunrise for Lakshman. Hanuman quickly moved towards the Himalayan Mountains by air. There was a charming hermitage on a hill in the middle of the forest. Some sages were performing fire sacrifices with great intensity. Some forced Hanuman to come down and meet the sages. One reason for his descent was personal and the other was professional.

On the personal front, it was because of his thirst. He had not had a chance to drink water for many days during the war. He was in dire need of water now and there was a sparkling river flowing next to the ashram. The other reason was that he had to reconfirm his route. Jambavan had named him Dronachal, the specific region in the Himalayan ranges from where the herbs were obtained. Surely these sages would know if he was flying in the right direction.

When he reached Dronachal Mountain. There were millions of herbs on the mountain. How did he understand which were the four herbs that Jambavan wanted him to bring? He lifted the entire Dronachal Mountain. He took a leap, heading towards the southern regions.

Hanuman introduced himself as a servant of Lord Rama. Bharata was extremely happy to meet an ally of his brother, whom he had not met for 13 years. Bharata began asking Hanuman innumerable questions about his brothers and their whereabouts. Hanuman explained to him that he didn't have enough time to answer his questions now as Lakshmana's life was in danger and he must return immediately to the mountain before it was too late.

Bharata understood Hanuman's distress due to lack of time. He felt that he had already caused enough grief to everyone in Ayodhya by being born as Kaikeyi's son. So he literally dragged Hanuman out of Ayodhya to Sumitra's palace. Hanuman left Ayodhya. Lifting the Dronachal Mountain, he shot an arrow into the sky, heading southwards with renewed vigour and determination.

As Hanuman approached the battlefield, the fragrance of various herbs began to spread rapidly in the air. As the fragrance wafted into Lakshman's nose, he regained consciousness.

All the monkeys who along with Lakshman had fallen unconsious on the battlefield woke up from deep sleep. What was a cause of celebration in the monkey army became a cause of despair in the demon army. This was because Ravana had thrown the bodies of the dead demons into the sea so that the enemies would never estimate his losses and would always be unaware of how much of his army was still alive in the protection of the palace. He looked foolish to see all the dead monkeys revive. Rama was very happy to see his brother alive again and embraced his brother with great love.

❐

***Raghupati Kinhi Bahut Badaai |***
***Tum Mam Priya Bharatahi Sam Bhai || 12***

[Lord Rama praised you a lot and said that you are as dear to him as his brother Bharat.]

## The Essence

Ayodhya was decorated with great pomp during the swayamvara ceremony of Hema, daughter of Kusha and granddaughter of Rama. This incident happened after Rama returned to Ayodhya. Chitrangada kidnapped the bride by releasing Mohnastra right in front of the full assembly which temporarily rendered her unconscious. Chitrangada disappeared. When they regained consciousness, the most powerful warriors of the army chased Chitrangada. The young prince defeated the entire Ayodhya army. Using Vayavastra he created a whirlwind effect. Hundreds of soldiers flew into the air.

At the same time King Ugrabahu also entered. Ugrabahu disarmed Luv and very soon Luv was left unconscious on the battlefield. With Luv unconscious, the entire Ayodhya army broke down.

Kusha intervened and controlled the situation. In a short while both father and son were taken captive. Kusha then turned his attention to his unconscious brother. The matter reached Lord Rama who in a surprising move freed his friend Ugrabahu from captivity and embraced him warmly. To reward Kusha for his bravery Rama gave him a divine bracelet which was gifted to him by sage Agastya. Kusha was very pleased to receive that gift from his father.

He wore the bracelet. Its radiance increased manifold. Kush immediately wanted to know more about the source of the bracelet. Agastya Rishi, who was also present there, told - "This bracelet was given by the sea god Varuna in return for a favor. Long ago a crowd of demons had taken shelter on the seafloor. No matter how hard Indra tried to find them they remained untraceable in the vast expanse of the sea. When Agastya Muni drank the water of the entire sea they were exposed. Finally they were killed by the gods. Agastya returned the water of the sea through another medium and thus the sea was restored. As a token of gratitude the sea god gifted this priceless bracelet to the sage."

Agastya gifted it to Rama. Rama gifted it to Kusha as a token of appreciation of his valor. The question remained about the revival of Luv.

Agastya Rishi immediately suggested - Hanuman should be sent to bring the *Mrit-Sanjeevani* herb from the ashram of Mudgal Rishi. Hanuman had learnt to identify the Mrit-Sanjeevani herbs very well. As soon as the herbs arrived, Luv woke up from his unconscious state. Rama was so grateful to Hanuman for helping Luv revive. Rama gifted another bracelet as a symbol.

Just before the Lanka war, Rama had a serious discussion with the monkey army.

Rama said- "If someone comes with the intention of dedicating his life in our service, then Rama will immediately accept him without considering his merit or demerit. Even if Ravana came, he would ignore all his misdeeds and give him shelter."

When Sugreeva took refuge, he got Kishkindha. When Bharat took refuge, he got Ayodhya. When Vibhishana took refuge, he became the king of Lanka after the war.

Someone asked- "What would you have done if Ravana had taken refuge at this time?"

Rama immediately replied- "We would have made him the king of Ayodhya."

Everyone was surprised to hear this. They kept looking at each other but no one had the courage to ask Rama why he would do so.

A monkey asked a question about Bharat- Where will Bharat get the throne?"

Rama said- "Bharat will be made the king of Vaikunth." The monkeys wanted to ask questions about Rama but before that question, the question arose that what should be asked from Rama?

Rama understood what the monkeys wanted to know. He looked towards the monkeys and said- "I will roam in all the three kingdoms, Ayodhya."

Hanuman was one of the most devoted souls, he was denied a position or a kingdom. Rama asked Hanuman- "O Hanuman! Whosoever came to my refuge, has received the kingdom from me. I could not give you a suitable gift. All those who have attained fortune, have received it by your grace only. You yourself have not received anything. I really want to bless you and sincerely fulfill your wishes. Serve Lanka, and Vaikuntha and all of them."

Hanuman smiled brightly. What was the secret behind that smile?

He told Rama- "The others whom I favoured have ruled only one kingdom. Whereas I have ruled two kingdoms."

Rama and all the monkeys were pleasantly surprised to hear this. How did Hanuman acquire the rule over not one but two kingdoms without anyone knowing?

Rama asked- "Over which two kingdoms do you have sovereignty?"

Hanuman bent down and touched his head to both the lotus feet of Lord Rama and said, "I am quite fortunate to have got the rule over these two kingdoms."

Rama was so pleased with Hanuman's loving reply that he embraced him with great love and appreciated his dedication and service.

One day Rama and the three brothers were in the gardens of Ayodhya along with their fifth brother Hanuman. After walking for a long time, Rama felt tired. He decided to rest under the shade of a huge tree in the garden itself. As Rama expressed his wish, everyone looked towards Hanuman and hoped that he would make the necessary arrangements for Rama's comfort. Hanuman turned around and kept looking at the sky. Seeing Hanuman thus discouraged, Lakshman himself spread a sheet on the grass for Rama and sat down near his head, gently placing it on his lap.

Bharat then looked at Hanuman and hoped that he would at least take some action now. But Hanuman seemed indifferent to whatever was happening. He was busy watching the birds and was unable to concentrate on anything. His heart was smiling. Bharat immediately sat down at Rama's feet, and placed his lotus feet on his thighs to gently massage them. Then Shatrughna turned to Hanuman and hoped to do some service to him. But Hanuman was still very busy, he was playing with the squirrels. Shatrughna sat down and started massaging Rama's arms.

As the three brothers got busy in their separate services to Rama, Hanuman immediately ran with a peacock fan to return in a little while. With great enthusiasm he used it to fan the four brothers. The cool refreshing breeze brought great comfort to everyone. Only then did the brothers understand Hanuman's mood and his mood was that why serve Rama alone when they can get the opportunity to serve all the four brothers whom he respect. No wonder Rama considered him as dear as his beloved brothers.

❐

***Sahasa Badan Tumharo Yash Gaavai |***
***As Kahi Shripati Kanth Lagaavai || 13***

[Saying that even a thousand-hooded snake will always sing your glory, Lord Rama embraced you.]

## The Essence

Kesari and Anjana did not know that their son Hanuman was in danger. Samasadan was killed by Kesari. The same Samasadan had a son- Vrikshasur. He heard about his father's death. He became restless to take revenge. When Hanuman was born, he thought that killing the enemy's child would be the right way to take revenge.

Vrikshasur had the boon of taking the form of a tree. He started thinking of killing Hanuman by taking the form of a tree. He had the special skill of catching the enemy with his shadow.

One day Hanuman had surrounded the whole sky. It was a good opportunity for Vrikshasur to get his shadow. He immediately caught hold of Hanuman and started pulling him towards himself. As soon as he pulled the shadow, Hanuman felt that some power was pulling him against his will.

Hanuman called out to his father "Father! Some invisible force is pulling me towards itself."

Kesari said- "Don't worry. I am coming." Kesari grabbed Hanuman and started pulling him towards himself. Kesari started pulling him back. Hanuman was being pulled from both sides and it was becoming difficult for him to bear the pain on both sides of the body. Hanuman reduced his size several times. As soon as this happened, the shadow also shrunk and Vrikshasur had to leave him.

Hanuman decided to teach Vrikshasur a lesson. He recognized the demon tree by surveying the area. As soon as Hanuman would go near the tree, the demon would catch his shadow and eat him. Hanuman decided to defeat the demon with his speed and picked up a big stone and ran towards the demon. The demon did not get a chance. Before the demon could understand anything, Hanuman thrust the stone in his mouth. Hanuman had miscalculated the size of the demon. That stone was not enough to stop the tree from swallowing Hanuman. The tree regained consciousness and caught Hanuman's shadow and Hanuman went straight into its mouth. Hanuman's tail got tied around the tree. Due to which the demon's plan to eat him was stopped.

The tail pulled the tree further and stopped the demon's plan to eat him. The more the demon pulled Hanuman, the more he himself got uprooted. Eventually the whole tree broke and fell to the ground and Hanuman was freed. This was the end of Vrikshasur. His father had died at the hands of Kesari and the son had died by Kesari's son's tail.

It is believed that the demon was killed not by Hanuman but by Hanuman's tail. Hanuman had realized long ago that his tail did not obey him like other monkeys.

Hanuman asked his father, "Why does my tail disobey me, father?"

The father gave valuable advice "A monkey should always respect his tail. Make friends with it."

From that day Hanuman started worshipping his tail and even called it his friend. The tail soon started responding to his thoughts.

The news of Hanuman's power had reached Ravana. Ravana was nervous. He feared that Hanuman's mighty power would ring his death knell. Many demons had lost their lives trying to kill Hanuman. Every trick of Ravana failed. Now it was Chakrasur's turn.

Ravana ordered Chakrasur, "Chakrasur! Enter Kesari's kingdom with full preparation and attack his son Hanuman."

As soon as Kesari came to know about Ravana's plan, Kesari and Anjana put Hanuman under house arrest.

Kesari instructed Hanuman, "It is a matter of a few days, son Hanuman. Do not go out to play. You have been attacked many times. We do not want any more trouble to arise." Anjana kissed Hanuman's forehead lovingly.

Hanuman obeyed his parents and stayed in his house.

Chakrasur, the storm demon, entered the monkey kingdom. It caused a lot of destruction. Kesari had gone out of the kingdom. Hanuman quietly ran away from home. Chakrasur saw Hanuman. He immediately caught him at the storm speed. He got trapped deeper and deeper in the storm.

Hanuman saw that when the demon passed over a pit, the storm demon did not enter it. He saw that the direction in which the demon was moving was clockwise. Hanuman started moving in the anti-clockwise direction. Which helped to trap the demon. Hanuman kept moving lower and lower until he could jump into a pit. The demon came above the pit and Hanuman jumped into it. The wise boy Hanuman was freed from the demon's captivity.

The demon kept wandering here and there for Hanuman. But he could not be found. Meanwhile the demon encountered Hanuman's friend. This friend had a damru (drum) given by Hanuman. Hanuman had received this toy from Vriksharaj, the monkey father of Sugriva and Bali. It was a magical damru.

It was made to protect Hanuman from any disaster. Hanuman had instructed his friend to play the damru whenever he was in trouble. Sensing Chakrasura's trouble, the monkey boy started playing the damru.

The strange sound of the damru pierced Chakrasura's ears. Chakrasura could not bear the torture anymore. He simply fell down in pain. Writhing on the ground, he died slowly and painfully.

Hanuman is an incarnation of Shiva. He has been blessed by all the gods multiple times. Rama and Sita have blessed him. He is so powerful that his name alone is enough to save one from all possible calamities and scare away negative elements. Everyone including the thousand-hooded snake sings in his praises.

❒

***Sankadik Brahmaadi Muneesa |***
***Narad Sarad Sahit Aheesa || 14***

[Sanaka and the great sages, Brahma, Narada, Saraswati and others praise you.]

## The Essence

Hanuman's childhood was spent in forests. Somewhere there were dense forests and somewhere there were gardens. Dangerous animals used to roam there. The noise of many types of animals and birds including tiger, tigress, lion, jackal, fox, etc. was always heard. Hanuman ji's childhood was spent in such a natural environment. Hanuman would play with such dangerous animals. He would enjoy it a lot. Hanuman had extraordinary energy. Tigers used to get tired after getting beaten up while playing with Hanuman. Hanuman would sit on them and ride.

Hanuman was very naughty in childhood. Joking with everyone was his daily routine. There was a special sage Trinbandhu. Hanuman ji would tease him a lot. One morning when the sage came out of his house, he saw that a tiger was tied to the door. The sage was frightened. He ran to the back door to get out of the house. He opened the door. There was a wild elephant with huge tusks tied up. He couldn't understand whose trick was this? Who had the strength to grapple with these wild animals and tie them to the pillars of his door?

It was the easiest task for Hanuman. The sage could not tolerate this mischief any more and he cursed Hanuman that this monkey child will forget all his powers until someone reminds him of them. He cursed Hanuman with immense love. This curse could not harm anyone. It was not a curse out of anger. It was a fatherly feeling to protect him from messing with more powerful sages.

Seeing such a brave child, the sages living in the nearby ashrams would like Hanuman ji very much. Hanuman ji's childhood attracted the great sages and saints. The sages could not stop themselves from feeling immense love for this little monkey. Hanuman somehow touched their hearts in a way that they could not understand.

One day Hanuman was meditating. Suddenly, he felt someone's touch on his shoulder. He opened his eyes and looked back to see Bali, the prince of Kishkindha standing there. Hanuman was surprised. Bali signaled Hanuman for a fight. Hanuman did not want to fight but to meditate. Seeing this, Bali started insulting Hanuman. Hanuman ji ignored Bali's words. Along with Hanuman, Bali also used abusive words for Rama, so Hanuman, irritated, accepted Bali's challenge. The next morning, a duel was decided by mutual consent in front of the entire kingdom.

The next morning Brahma appeared and requested Hanuman to use only one-tenth of his energy in the fight against Bali. Hanuman accepted Brahma's request. Hanuman went to the wrestling arena. Bali used the necklace of mystic gems he had with him to absorb half of Hanuman's energy. Bali was unable to handle even half of Hanuman's power. His veins burst. Blood started flowing from his body. Seeing Bali helpless, Brahma instructed Bali to release his drawn energy immediately. Bali was told not to wrestle. Seeing his condition getting serious, Bali released his energy. Now Hanuman started moving away from Bali.

He fell unconscious after a short distance. When Bali regained consciousness, he was sitting in front of Brahma. Bali asked him why he was unable to absorb Hanuman's power. Brahma explained that Hanuman had used one-tenth of his regular power as per his instructions. Hanuman is an incarnation of Lord Shiva. As an avatar, Hanuman's powers are infinitely greater than yours. Bali was surprised to hear this.

According to another legend, Kesari once fought a duel with a hunter. The hunter defeated Kesari in a few moments. Anjana was surprised to see this. Anjana had seen Kesari fight many times with powerful demons. But she had never seen him get defeated easily. She closed her eyes and meditated on Lord Shiva. When she opened her eyes, Lord Shiva was standing before her in the hunter's attire. Anjana offered some flowers and bowed down to him. Following his mother, Hanuman also collected some flowers and offered them at the feet of his new teacher Lord Shiva. Kesari apologized for his foolishness.

Lord Shiva accepted Hanuman's offer to teach him. When Shiva touched his ring to the child Hanuman's tongue, the child Hanuman magically started praying in praise of the Lord. Shiva uttered the secret Pranava mantra in Hanuman's right ear. Hanuman became fully enlightened. Shiva told Hanuman- "Very soon Goddess Saraswati, the goddess of learning, will bless him with unlimited wisdom. Not only this, but when the right time comes, she will also give him proficiency in music.

Over time, Hanuman's wisdom and learning ability increased incredibly. On Saraswati's insistence, Hanuman reached Kishkindha at night. Hanuman heard Narada singing and playing the Veena. Seeing Hanuman's curiosity, Narada inspired him towards music. Soon Hanuman became proficient in all possible musical instruments like singing, music, tavla, flute, etc.

The story related to Narada and Hanuman is interesting and informative. Narada decided to test his disciple. He ordered Hanuman to sing his favorite song. The obedient Hanuman started singing. Narada was mesmerized by his voice. Due to the effect of Hanuman's singing, the stones started melting and flowing. When the singing stopped, the melted stones became hard. Narada's Veena fell into the river during this time. To get it, Narada requested Hanuman to sing once again.

Now Hanuman had a mischievous smile on his face. He refused to sing. This was the only Veena Narada had. Hanuman started to move away from Narada and then started running away from him. Narada had no choice but to chase Hanuman. Hanuman started moving around the city of Kishkindha. Finally Hanuman came back to the same place from where he had started. Hanuman sang a song obeying his Guru's request. The rocks melted. Veena was back. Narada asked Hanuman "Why did you make me run so much to get the Veena?"

Hanuman smiled and said, "I wanted to sanctify the entire city of Kishkindha with the dust of his Guru's lotus feet." Narada was mesmerized by the answer. He was very impressed by Hanuman's humility and creative thinking.

❐

***Yam Kuber Dikpal Jahan Te |***
***Kavi Kovid Kahi Sakai Kahan Te || 15***

[Yama, Kubera, the protectors of all directions, poets and scholars cannot truly describe your glory even if they want to.]

## The Essence

Hanuman didn't have to bring Sanjivani herb. Probably he was not aware that he would bring the herb easily from the Himalayas. Tulsidas ji has tried to make it clear here that in those times Yama and Kubera were deployed to protect the herbs so that no one misuses them. Here Hanuman ji faced Yama and Kubera.

There is no rest in the life of a warrior. He has to be always alert. He has to be ready for war. Hanuman had not yet recovered from the long, difficult and tiring journey from Lanka to the Himalayas when he got a new challenge. Hanuman got ready for a duel with his invisible enemy. Due to the dense fog or excess of clouds, Hanuman could not see anyone. Whoever had kicked him was hiding behind that fog.

As soon as the fog cleared, a scary person appeared before him. Seeing him Hanuman said- "O Mrityudev! I cannot believe that it is you! Why did you kick me?"

"O Vayu Putra! Forgive me for unintentionally kicking a gentleman like you." Yama said with folded hands. Hanuman remained calm. He did not reply. Yama continued his story and said- "I myself had given you a boon that you will never be able to touch death. I was fastened to this mountain with the shackles of Rudra mantras and I was instructed to kill anyone who dares to step on this mountain. No matter how hard I try, I am not able to free myself from this bond."

Hanuman felt pity for Yama. With one touch, the shackles of Rudra mantra broke and Yama was freed. It was Ravana who had made security arrangements for these herbs. Hanuman was impressed by this foresight and strategy of Ravana.

Yama thanked Hanuman a lot and blessed him. Hanuman blessed him with fearlessness. Yama said to Hanuman- "Whoever remembers you will never fear death. Whoever follows Hanuman, Yama himself will protect him."

As Hanuman prepared to go to Lanka after saving Yama, he heard a voice. He stopped.

It was a very faint voice. Hanuman moved towards where the voice was coming from. The voice became clear. This clear voice was coming from a cave in the mountain. There was a sense of desperation in the voice. Hanuman entered the cave. He was welcomed.

The person hanging from the roof of the cave humbly requested- "Please help me!"

This was a person held captive by Ravana. Hanuman removed the chains on the roof and carefully brought down the person. Hanuman turned him around, then suddenly he exclaimed "Shani Dev you."

Shani Dev told Hanuman with folded hands, "Being an astrologer, Ravana knew the power of my gaze. He knew that I cast a favourable gaze on a person for two and a half years and an unfavourable gaze for the next two and a half years. When Ravana came to my abode, astrologically I was favouring Ravana. Ravana imprisoned me to ensure that I do not stare at him at all in the future. That is, there is no question of unfavourable gaze.

Ravana wanted to ensure that I do not cast an unfavourable gaze not only on him but on anyone in Lanka, even on any object in Lanka. So Ravana confined me in this cave on the edge of Lanka. This cave is such that if someone looks from outside, he can see only the wall and nothing else."

Shani expressed his gratitude to Hanuman. Shani blessed him that whoever remembers Hanuman will never be affected by the troubles caused by Shani's gaze. Many such stories are popular.

❒

***Tum Upkaar Sugreevahin Keenha |***
***Rama Milaaye Raajpad Deenha || 16***

[You helped Sugreeva by introducing him to Lord Rama who then helped him regain his kingship.]

## The Essence

It is believed that in Treta Yuga, the Lord helped Sugreeva, the son of Surya and killed Bali, the son of Indra. In Dvapara Yuga, He helped Arjuna, the son of Indra and killed Karna, the son of Surya. In Dvapara Yuga, Arjuna was humble and Karna was arrogant. In Treta Yuga, Sugreeva was humble while Bali was full of arrogance.

Sugreeva was physically weak. He was also weak in character. He had no courage. He couldn't ask for favours. This is where Hanuman comes into Sugreeva's life. Hanuman was that pious person.

Hanuman introduced Sugreeva to the Lord. There are three categories of people in this world-

1. Materialists,
2. Sadhaks (those who are on the path of spiritual perfection), and
3. Siddhas (those who have completed the path of spirituality).

Materialists are least likely to reach God. Sugreeva is one such materialist. Hanuman is a Siddha Purush. He has reached perfection.

Hanuman completed his education from the Sun. He wanted to give his Guru Dakshina. It is also a form of donation. The Sun had asked for a pledge from Hanuman as a donation. That pledge was- 'Hanuman should take care of his son Sugreeva and serve him.' Hanuman immediately gave the pledge. From then on Hanuman remained with Sugreeva in every moment of happiness and sorrow. Not only this, but he also introduced him to Rama. This was no less than a favor.

Every character of Ramayana written by Maharishi Valmiki definitely gives a message. Hanuman is a symbol of hope for others. In times of crisis, if a friend or stranger says, "Don't worry. We are here", then the morale of the troubled person boosts up. Hanuman ji is still revered. Hanuman is the savior of Sugreeva and Rama.

Hanuman is not only the savior of Sugreeva and Rama, but he is always ready to help all those who are in fear. Once Hanuman assured the scared monkeys - "Now there is no fear of Bali on this mountain. As long as I stand by your side, there is nothing to fear. Matang Rishi is by your side. Now Bali cannot pose any danger to you on this mountain."

He suggested to the monkeys that they should use the trick of disguise so that they can find out the intentions of these personalities. They should take the form of a traveling hermit. No pious soul can possibly hide his intentions from a saintly soul. Through this, use your expertise of reading human minds by analyzing human psychology.

Hanuman ji himself took the form of a hermit and set out to identify the two strangers. There was a brief conversation and Hanuman easily understood that they were not enemies but friends. Who were these two strangers? They were Rama and Lakshmana. This incident increased the confidence of the other monkeys. After a brief conversation with Hanuman, Rama understood that Hanuman cannot be a hermit and neither can he be an ordinary person. Hanuman's first impression on Rama was deep. Rama looked at Hanuman and whispered in Lakshman's ear - "After meeting him, I am completely convinced that Sugreeva is the right person to help us find Sita."

Hanuman took Rama and Lakshman to Sugreeva. He made three friends. Rama met Sugreeva. Sugreeva had a simple heart. He was so simple that he didn't hesitate in telling Rama all his shortcomings. He makes his name meaningful. The word Sugreeva means - neck. A humble person always stands with his head bowed. A special quality of Sugreeva was his humility. Hanuman was the link between the Lord and his devotee.

Laxmana asked Rama to clear his doubts- "Why did you choose Sugreeva and not Bali to search for Sita?"

Rama cleared Lakshmana's doubts by telling him- "Sugreeva has two unique powers. One is that he is fast in running. Second is that he is very resourceful. He can live on Rishimukh Mountain and not Bali. These powers are the right qualities to find Sita."

Hanuman not only helped Rama but he also helped Sugreeva gain the kingdom. This is why Tulsidas says- *Tum Upkaar Sugreevahi Keenha Rama Milaai Rajpada Dinha.*

❑

***Tumhro Mantra Vibhishan Mana |***
***Lankeshwar Bhae Saba Jaga Jana || 17***

[Similarly, following your teachings, Vibhishan also became the king of Lanka.]

## The Essence

Hanuman searched for Sita everywhere. He searched inside houses and inside temples.

Hanuman considered every house in Lanka as a temple. But Sita was not found. From one house Hanuman heard the sound of chanting of the holy name. Hanuman was pleased. Vibhishan welcomed Hanuman. Hanuman said- "Jai Shri Ram." Vibhishan asked Hanuman to introduce himself. Hanuman introduced himself, "I am Hanuman, son of Pavan. I am the servant of Rama."

Vibhishan told Hanuman about the dangers of being a devotee among demons. He did his sadhna in hiding, fearing dreadful consequences if caught. Hanuman asked Vibhishan, "Why don't you leave Lanka and take refuge in Lord Rama?"

Vibhishan took a deep breath and said, "How can I leave my brother? After all, he is my brother. Lanka is my home."

Hanuman lovingly explained to Vibhishan, "It all depends on who you think you are. What is your swadharma? If you think you are Ravana's brother. Your dharma is to stay in Lanka, to be Ravana's advisor. This indicates a relationship. On the contrary, if you think you are my brother, from the family of Rama and Sita, then this is your spiritual knowledge. So you can leave

Lanka. Take refuge in Rama. Dharma is always dynamic, not static. It changes with the understanding of who you really are."

Vibhishan was overwhelmed by Hanuman's enlightening words. Vibhishan promised Hanuman that he would consider his proposal.

After Hanuman left, Ravana entered Vibhishan's palace. He said angrily, "Vibhishan! I have to face constant embarrassment because of you. You are a blot on our respected demon clan."

Vibhishan asked in surprise, "What have I done that the demon clan is disgraced?"

"Whatever you do is unforgivable. You keep reciting the name of Rama continuously. Which demon does this? Why are you hell-bent on behaving like a heavenly citizen instead of a true demon?"

"Oh!" Vibhishan felt relieved and said- "So that's it. I can explain it. I am not chanting the name of God. I am actually chanting your name. 'Ra' is the short form of my respected elder brother Ravana and 'Ma' is the short form of my respected Mandodari Bhabhi. I constantly chant your name. The chant of Ravana Mandodari is quite long. I have invented a short form of it, Ra-Ma."

On hearing this, Ravana's anger subsided. He kept smiling while standing.

Vibhishan was looking for this opportunity. He immediately said to Ravana- "I want you and every citizen of Lanka to fill your walls with 'Rama'."

Ravan liked this proposal of Vibhishan. He happily ordered- "You get my name written on every wall of Lanka. Pass an order to every citizen of Lanka to chant Rama's name from today. This is my order." Saying this, Ravana left from there.

This was the effect of Hanuman ji's proposal which the intelligent Vibhishan presented before Ravana very well and convinced him to chant Rama's name in Lanka. Hanuman devotee Tulsidas ji happily wrote- Vibhishan refuses your mantra. Sita's presence in Lanka was an important question. This subject was being seriously considered in Lanka. Ravana's ministers could not go against him.

They could not speak against him. Ravana liked flattery. He was always surrounded by flatterers. No one had the courage to give good advice to Ravana. Apart from Vibhishan, Ravana was not a well-wisher. In the discussion about Sita, all the members of the assembly had left the decision to Ravana. After this deliberation, it became clear to Vibhishan that it would be beneficial to accept Hanuman's words. Vibhishan decided that he would follow his spiritual Dharma, the supreme Dharma.

Vibhishan explained to Ravana, "It would be a just decision to let go of Sita. It is a sin to kidnap and forcefully take someone else's wife. It is not befitting for a king to behave like this."

On hearing this, Ravana expelled Vibhishan from his court and Lanka. Vibhishan was extremely happy even after being insulted. He left the court. He believed that this blow of Ravana's feet would take him to the other pair of feet.

A spiritual mindset is better than a materialistic mindset. Vibhishan left Lanka with his four trusted friends and reached Rama's camp across the ocean and informed the guard of the monkey army that he had come to Rama's refuge. Everyone was stunned by Vibhishan's arrival.

Sugreeva was not keen to include the enemy's brother in his camp. He said clearly, "O Lord, it is foolish to let the enemy enter our camp. He can reveal all our military secrets. How can we trust a person who is betraying his own brother?"

Rama looked at Hanuman and asked. "What do you say Hanuman? Sugreeva and I trust your opinion so we will do as you say."

Hanuman told everyone about his conversation with Vibhishan in Lanka. He told that Vibhishan was the only holy man he had met in the whole of Lanka who used to chant the names of the Lord despite all the odds.

Vibhishan didn't expect Rama to take his advice. Lakshmana was openly not in his favour. Rama said, "Vibhishan! We will try whatever you say." Vibhishan was pleased.

❒

***Yug Sahasra Yojana Par Bhaanu |***
***Lilyo Taahi Madhur Phala Jaanu || 18***

[Though the sun was standing at a distance of thousands of yojanas, you mistook it for a sweet fruit and swallowed.]

## The Essence

Numbers have importance in the life of all of us. The entire life of any person is based on numbers. Similarly, the calculation of the entire universe has been done in numbers. It is happening even today and will continue to happen in the future. Tulsidas ji knew the distance of the sun from the earth from the ancient sages and saints. On that basis, he has mentioned in this *choupai* by telling the distance of the sun from the earth that Hanuman ji, in his childhood, mistook the sun situated at a distance of 15,36,00,000 kilometers as a sweet fruit and put it in his mouth. According to modern astronomical scientists, the average distance between the earth and the sun is about 15 crore kilometers. At present, astronomers consider the distance of the sun from the earth to be 14,96,00,000 kilometers and in miles it is 92,96,00,000 miles.

In ancient times, our scientists would do the calculations in 'yojanas' and not in kilometers or miles. Let us understand how to convert Yojana into kilometer or mile -

Statisticians believe that Yuga is equal to 12000 years. On this basis, one Sahasra is equal to 1000 years. Mathematicians consider one Yojana to be equal to 8 miles and do further calculations. For this, they developed a formula. For example -

"Yuga × Sahasra × Yojana = Bhanu", Bhanu means the Sun. Putting the numbers in this formula - "Yuga 12000 × Sahasra 1000 × Yojana 8 = Bhanu 96000000 miles", this means that the distance of the Sun from the Earth is - 96000000 miles.

Now let us calculate according to the knowledge of modern youth because nowadays everyone understands distance in kilometers very well. Today one mile is considered equal to 1.6 kilometers. So 96,000,000 miles × 1.6 km = 15,36,00,000 km. There is a slight difference between the distances known by ancient Indian sages and the distances told by modern astronomers. The slight difference does not matter much because today the calculations are done through the most modern technology whereas in ancient times mechanical equipment like today were not available.

Annaprashan ceremony (grain initiation) of infant Hanuman was organized. Hanuman first ate some grains and his hunger was activated. His mother fed him every possible fruit. Child Hanuman's hunger was not getting satiated. Narad Muni pointed towards the Sun.

Hanuman leaped towards the Sun thinking it to be a big fruit. The story of infant Hanuman leaping to swallow the Sun is often seen as hunger of the stomach. Scholars consider it to be hunger of the heart to acquire knowledge. It is an indication of his eagerness to acquire infinite knowledge. Hanuman was a very hungry child. His hunger was not like the hunger of ordinary children. His hunger was intellectual hunger. It was a hunger to understand the deeper truths of life. Tulsidas ji has presented Hanuman ji's thirst for knowledge in a new form and has also explained the distance between the earth and the moon through Hanuman ji.

❐

***Prabhu Mudrika Meli Mukha Mahee |***
***Jaladhi Langhi Gaye Achraj Naahi || 19***

[By taking Lord Rama's ring in your mouth, you crossed the ocean and it was no wonder in that.]

## The Essence

Sugreeva called a special meeting with Rama and Lakshman to find a way to search Sita. All the distinguished persons of Kishkindha were invited to this meeting. After discussion it was decided to send the Vanar Sena in different directions to search for Sita. So the monkeys were divided into different groups. Necessary information and instructions were given regarding each direction.

Sugreeva included Hanuman in the group going south. This group was led by Angad. Jambavan and others were appointed to assist him.

Addressing the southern group, Sugreeva said to Hanuman, "Jambavan is wise. You are the power of Angad who carries everyone along. The success of Sita search depends on you. No obstacle on land can stop you. Be it sea or sky, you are capable of crossing all. No one in the three worlds can match your skill, cleverness, adventurous spirit or intelligence. You will surely succeed in finding Sita."

Rama gave a gold ring to Hanuman. He held the ring between the index finger and thumb of his right hand and placed it on his head reverently. Hanuman safely hid the ring in his waistband. Taking Rama's blessings, he set out for the search expedition with the ring in his hand. Keeping in mind the difficult journey, Hanuman kept the ring safe in his mouth.

The idea of crossing the 800 mile sea was discussed. Then Jambavan reminded Hanuman of his powers. And no one was able to cross the sea and come back. Rama gave the ring only to Hanuman. If anyone could cross the ocean, it was Hanuman.

Hanuman himself is Pavanputra. He involved the air element. The jump was over the ocean, so the water element was involved. He used the sky route and thus the sky element was involved. Sita had to be found to be Bhumi Suta or daughter of the earth, so the earth element was also involved. Hanuman had the knowledge of the Panchtatva. The burning of Lanka involved the fire element as well.

Hanuman faced four obstacles while crossing the ocean. The first obstacle was a golden mountain named Mayanaka. It arose from the depths of the ocean. The deity of that mountain invited Hanuman to rest. Hanuman refused this invitation.

The name of the obstacle was Surasa. She was sent by the gods to test Hanuman's preparations for Lanka. She rose from the ocean and blocked Hanuman's path saying that she had a boon from Brahma that anyone who would pass across the ocean would have to enter her mouth. Surasa reacted by increasing the size of her mouth to stop his forward movement. This angered Hanuman and he increased his size assuming he was bigger than her. Surasa defeated him in size and then Hanuman grew even bigger. She once again defeated Hanuman. He not only became small but also very small. Hanuman became very small and entered her mouth and came out, thus fulfilling Brahma's boon. Surasa was impressed by his intelligence and in return blessed him to be victorious.

Suddenly, he was pulled towards the ocean with great force. He fell into the open mouth of a demoness named Singhika who could capture anyone with her shadow. She swallowed Hanuman whole in a single gulp. Hanuman tore open her stomach from inside and came out of the bloody water and once again headed towards Lanka in the sky.

Hanuman reached Lanka on the other side of the ocean. The fourth obstacle to be crossed was Lankini, the head of security of Lanka. When Hanuman tried to go inside she pushed him out forcefully. An angry Hanuman punched her. Lankini left the service of her false guru Ravana and started serving her true guru Rama. Though this journey was difficult for anyone, Hanuman completed his journey with ease.

❒

***Durgam Kaaj Jagat Ke Jete |***
***Sugam Anugraha Tumhare Tete || 20***

[By your grace, all the difficult tasks of the world become easy.]

## The Essence

Before crossing the ocean Hanuman ji had many questions in his mind. Hanuman ji asked Jambvant- "Tell me! What should I do after going to Lanka? Should I drink this ocean from here itself? Should I lift Lanka and throw it in the ocean along with the Trikuta Mountain? Should I catch the evil Ravana and crush him with my feet like an insect? Should I wipe out the name of demons from the world?"

Once Hanuman had asked many such questions to Rama also. "O Lord!" If you permit, should I bring nectar from heaven or hell? Should I catch the moon and squeeze it in his mouth like a wet cloth? If Yamraj does something wrong, should I catch him and chew him raw? Why not catch the sun and lock him in hell so that he cannot rise?

What it means is that Hanuman ji was capable enough of doing the most impossible tasks. This is the reason why Tulsidas has written for Hanuman in these words-*Durgam Kaaj Jagat Ke Jete.*

Hanuman ji found Sita in Ashok Vatika and gave her Rama's message. With Sita's blessings and permission, Hanuman ji proceeded to make a round of the city of Lanka. He saw Yoginis who were hailing Ravana. Roaring in anger, he jumped into the midst of the Yoginis, frightening them. While pacifying the frightened followers, one of them asked Hanuman, "O monkey! Who are you? And how did you come here?"

Hanuman introduced himself and said, "My name is Hanuman. I am the son of the wind god. I have accepted the slavery of Lord Rama by whose mercy I can destroy the entire earth including the seas and forests. I have come here in search of Mother Sita, who has been held captive by the evil Ravana. Who are you and why are you wishing for the victory of a sinner like Ravana?"

One of the Yoginis replied, "I am the daughter of the Chandaswarupa Himalaya. I am also known as Parvati and Kali. Ravana has won me by his devotion because of which I protect him from his enemies. O monkey! Please show me your huge form which you were boasting about some time ago."

Hanuman showed his huge size to the followers. The Yoginis were left wide-mouthed seeing Hanuman's huge size. Remove your anger and tell me what I can do for you. Hanuman assumed his original form and said- "O divine goddess! I request you to leave Lanka at this very moment. Why do you want the victory of the sinful Ravana? If he does not die then there will be uproar in the entire universe."

The Goddess replied, "The one who insulted Sita has insulted me also. I will leave Lanka as you say."

Hanuman said,"O Parvatnandini Maheshwari! You are worshipped by the great trinity, Brahma, Vishnu and Mahesh. You are the great illusory energy. You sustain this material world. Bless Rama with victory. Help him destroy Ravana"

Goddess Chandika blessed Rama and said "Rama will surely conquer Ravana. Will shine as the Sun of the glorious Ikshvaku dynasty. He has my full blessings to destroy Ravana. O Hanuman! The Gods are grateful to any person who pleases them."

After this Chandika left Lanka. Hanuman returned to Ashok Vatika.

Hanuman ji was finally caught by Indrajit and his tail was set on fire, then he set the whole Lanka on fire and set it on fire while offering incense and lamps to the Goddess. After completing his work Hanuman went to Mata Sita to seek her blessings. After this Hanuman crossed the ocean. He gave Sita's message to Rama.

Vibhishan told Rama that Brahma Ji had given Ravana a boon that even if his limbs were cut, they would be joined immediately. Thus his body could never be destroyed. Technically he had ensured Ravana's immortality. While giving this boon, Brahma Ji had also given him a special arrow. He warned Ravana that his life was literally within this arrow. If this arrow hit his navel, it would immediately destroy all his power. Vibhishan said that the only person other than Ravana who knew the whereabouts of that arrow was Mandodari. Who can take this arrow from Mandodari?

Who will make this impossible possible? Hanuman said, "He can try."

Taking Rama's blessings, Hanuman jumped towards the inner sanctum of Lanka. Hanuman started walking slowly with the help of a stick as an old, weak and wise astrologer. All the demons of Lanka started coming to this old Jyotish Acharya to know the future of their family members. Whatever this old astrologer would tell was so accurate that soon this news spread all over Lanka. This reached Mandodari's ears. She was devastated. She was worried about her husband's safety. She had almost lost them all. She wanted to know if there was a procedure that would ensure her victory.

Finally, he declared that today was the day of doom. Either Ravana would rule forever, or he would die. The mention of death sent a shiver down Mandodari's spine.

Hanuman said, "Let him not give this arrow to anyone, not even Brahma himself." He assured Mandodari that he was her well-wisher. She then asked the astrologer if there was a better place to keep the arrow than the glass pillar in which he had embedded it. The astrologer pointed to the pillar and it suddenly broke into pieces with a thundering sound, accompanied by a loud exclamation of "Jai Shri Ram." Shocked, Mandodari watched as Hanuman jumped out of the window, grasping the secret arrow in his hand. That marked the end of Ravana.

❐

***Ram Duware Tum Rakhvaare |***
***Hot Na Aagya Binu Paisaare || 21***

[You are the gatekeeper of Lord Rama, and no one can enter without your permission.]

## The Essence

The leaders of the monkey army including Rama and Lakshman gathered around Vibhishan. He shared with them the problem ahead. It was not a single but a double-edged problem. The name of the problem was Ahiravan Mahiravan. These were two cruel magician friends of Ravana who would take great pleasure in luring innocent people into their sinister traps and then offer them as human sacrifices. Vibhishan warned the monkey chieftains that dealing with these two meant dealing with a lot of treachery. Both the brothers could change their form at will and could do any trick possible or impossible in the blink of an eye. Now the primary goal was to ensure that Rama and Lakshmana remained safe.

Equipped with arms, the monkey army formed circular layers to protect Rama and Lakshman. With his tail, Hanuman made another strong wall around the concentric wall of monkeys. Only a small entrance was left through which only one person could go in or out. Hanuman himself stood guard over it. Vibhishan kept moving around the wall and Hanuman stood at the door. This is: *Ram duware tum rakhwaare hot na aagya binu paisaare.*

Hanuman stood guard at the door of Lord Rama and no one could enter without his consent. An elderly majestic king approached Hanuman. Introduced himself as Dasharatha, the father of Rama and Lakshman. He asked for permission to spend some time with his sons. Hanuman didn't want to disrespect Dasharatha either so he requested the king to wait a little till Vibhishan came. Dasharatha left in a hurry saying that he would return soon. Confused Hanuman told the incident to Vibhishan who warned Hanuman that even if his father Kesari came then do not let him in without his permission. Vibhishan was very pleased with Hanuman's vigilance.

After meeting Hanuman, Vibhishan started moving around the camp. In a few minutes he suddenly returned. Hanuman was surprised. Vibhishan asked Hanuman to allow him to enter the gate to inspect the situation inside. Hanuman obeyed and Vibhishan entered quickly. After some time Vibhishan came to the gate again. How was this possible? How could he come out when he had already come inside? Hanuman first thought that it was the imposter Ahiravana or Mahiravana.

When Vibhishan gave him some solid evidence Hanuman panicked realizing that he had sent the imposter inside. Both went inside and found that every single monkey inside was lying unconscious and both Ram and Lakshman were missing. The question was where were they now? Starting to search, they saw a pit. Hanuman immediately jumped into that pit. This pit was the way to Pataal Lok.

Hanuman transformed himself into a common monkey. There he heard a woman talking to someone that today there is a big celebration inside the palace where the king will perform a human sacrifice for the happiness of Goddess Mahamaya. Hanuman immediately entered the palace assuming a very small form.

Here Hanuman encountered a strange creature. His face was like that of a monkey and body like that of a crocodile.

Both fought. Hanuman tied that half monkey half crocodile with ropes and threw him on the ground. Then that protector introduced himself as Makaradhwaj, son of Hanuman. This unexpected introduction bewildered Hanuman who was never married. How could he have a son whom he didn't know about? When questioned. Makaradhwaj told that when Hanuman had burnt Lanka and then dipped his tail in the ocean to extinguish the fire, a drop of sweat had fallen into the ocean, which was swallowed by a female crocodile. Makaradhwaj was born from that crocodile. Hanuman was pleased to meet his son and Makaradhwaj promised to help his father find Rama and destroy all the evils of Ravana.

Makaradhwaj suggested Hanuman to meet the Nagakanya Chitrasena. She had many secrets of the demon brothers and she could surely help Hanuman find a solution. Hanuman entered Chitrasena's room in the form of a small bumble bee and attracted Chitrasena's attention. He showed her his original form. In the beginning, Chitrasena did not believe Hanuman. Hanuman had assumed his real form. Chitrasena agreed to help Hanuman on one condition. Her condition was that Rama would have to marry her in return for the favor.

A helpless Hanuman agreed to her condition but put a condition that Rama would marry her only if their bed could bear Rama's weight. Chitrasena agreed.

Chitrasena revealed some of the evil brothers' dark secrets. Mahiravana had once saved the life of a group of bees. Whenever a brother was killed in battle, the bees would fly and sprinkle heavenly nectar in his mouth, which could revive the dead. As long as these bees were alive, the brothers would live. Hanuman was attentively listening to Chitrasena.

One important thing Chitrasena told Hanuman was that the life of both the brothers is only partially present in their bodies.

The life of Ahiravana is stored in a large diamond. The life of Mahiravana is stored in five lamps which were continuously burning in five adjacent caves in the nearby mountain.

After knowing the secret Hanuman again took the form of a bumblebee and set out to find the whereabouts of the bees. He killed all the bees in that hive one by one. Only one bee survived. Helplessly, it took refuge in Hanuman and promised to help him in every possible way. Hanuman instructed the bee to go to Chitrasena. He went to the temple of Goddess Mahamaya i.e. Kamakshi Devi. He explained the whole situation to her. The Goddess blessed Hanuman to save the lives of Rama and Lakshmana.

After this, he reached Hanuman cave and started extinguishing the lamps in the five caves one by one. When he would extinguish one lamp, the previous lamp would light up again. It was necessary to extinguish all five together. The problem was that the caves were in five different directions. Hanuman assumed a five-headed form. He assumed the face of Varaha towards the north, Narasimha face towards the south, Garuda towards the west, Hanuman's original face towards the east and Hayagriva or horse face towards the top and extinguished all the five lamps together in one stroke. At the same time, Lakshman broke the diamond. Thus, both the demon brothers were permanently destroyed. Returning to Rama and Lakshman, Hanuman touched their feet and they embraced him in joy.

Chitrasena was happy. As Rama sat on the bed, it broke. Chitrasena thought it was Hanuman's trick. Rama explained to her that in this life he had taken a monogamous vow and thus he could not marry anyone other than Sita.

Ram assured Chitrasena that as Krishna he would certainly marry her. She would be one of his chief queens named Satyabhama. Chitrasena agreed. Rama then crowned

Makaradhwaj as the king of Pataal Loka. Makaradhwaj handed over the responsibilities of the kingdom to his ministers and went with them to help his father. The monkeys cheered loudly when they saw Hanuman returning safely with Ram and Lakshman.

❒

***Sab Sukh Lahai Tumhari Sarana |***
***Tum Rakshak Kahu Ko Darana || 22***

[All happiness is attained by coming under your shelter. When you are the protector, then what is there to fear?]

## The Essence

There is some story behind every couplet of Hanuman Chalisa. It is said that the Brahmins of Kanyakubj had control over about 4,400 villages. These Brahmins claimed that Lord Rama had gifted their ancestors with Hanuman as a witness. The Brahmins didn't have a single proof. Because of this, King Kumarpal didn't believe them. The Brahmins were deprived of all the villages.

Where should the Brahmins bring the proof? This was the real question. There was only one solution, which was to find Rama or Hanuman. Three thousand Brahmins set out on a journey to the south on foot to prove their claim.

The journey was difficult. They kept moving forward by eating fruits, crossing dense forests, rivers and difficult areas. A time came when everyone's mind and body became weak. They were unable to move forward. The helpless Brahmins prayed to Rama for help. One day an old yogi came in place of Rama. The Brahmins told him about the purpose of finding Rama. The Brahmins were pleased with the yogi's assurance.

The yogi made all the Brahmins sleep on a rock after flattening it. While they were asleep, Hanuman lifted the rock and took them back to their homeland in a matter of hours.

When the Brahmins woke up in the morning, Hanuman told the Brahmins, "Go back to Kanyakubja. Tell the king that I have instructed him to return the land to you. If he refuses, remove the hair from the left pouch. Use it once the king apologizes and promises to return your land. Follow the instructions carefully. You will get your land back."

Hanuman took out a hair from his right armpit and kept it in a pouch. Then he took out another hair from his left armpit and kept it in a separate pouch. Hanuman wrapped both the bags with tree bark and handed them over to the Brahmins.

The Brahmins were surprised to find themselves back home. They thanked Hanuman profusely. They left for the palace to tell the king about Hanuman's instructions. The king only laughed at them and said, "You expect me to believe that you met Hanuman?" He ridiculed them. "Now get lost!"

The Brahmins dropped the hair from the bag in the left armpit. The king sneered even more. The Brahmins left the palace. They had taken a few steps when suddenly they looked back and saw smoke rising from the palace. The next moment the palace caught fire. The fire didn't spread anywhere else. They were not surprised to see the king trying to save his life. The king pleaded with them to stop the fire and take the land. The Brahmins dropped the hair from the second bag and the fire disappeared. The palace was restored to its original state.

The king issued an order to return the land to the Brahmins saying that this land belonged to them forever. He now had enough evidence to believe this. The Brahmins could only thank Hanuman for giving them shelter and returning their life, their home and happiness. Hanuman never disappointed his devotees.

There is a reference to another incident. A man was roaming around in the battlefield. Who is he? No one knows. It was found that he is a resident of Pataal Lok. It was expected that this person would be a demon of Ravana. Perhaps he had invited a terrible demon named Bhasmalochan. Ravana was disturbed after the death of his brother Kumbhakarna. Bhasmalochan appeared on the battlefield with confidence. His eyes were also blindfolded. Bhasmalochan could burn with his sight. Suddenly there was chaos in the monkey army.

Ram's generals thought about what steps should be taken for safety. Then Bhasmalochan opened his eyes. His eyes were shining like the sun in its full glory. Seeing the mass destruction, Hanuman started running in the opposite direction using his intelligence. Seeing this, the monkeys got scared. No one understood why Hanuman was running in the opposite direction? If Hanuman himself is running in the opposite direction, then what will happen to us monkeys? Such thoughts were flashing in the minds of the monkeys.

Everyone was more curious about Hanuman's next move. Hanuman swiftly threw his tail in the air and hit Bhasmalochana's head with the iron board tied to the tail. There was an explosion and Bhasmalochana turned into a heap of ashes. What the monkeys were mistaking to be a piece of iron from a distance was actually a mirror. Hanuman showed the mirror to Bhasmalochana to see himself. Such is our protector Hanuman.

❒

***Aaapan Tej Samhaaro Aapai |***
***Tino Lok Haank Te Kanpai || 23***

[You alone can control your immense power, and even the three worlds tremble with your roar.]

## The Essence

It is clear from the birth story of Hanuman that his parents Kesari and Anjana were blessed by the sages that their child will shake the three worlds. There is a story related to this blessing. One day Anjana was meditating in a cave in a secluded mountain. When she opened her eyes, she saw a very scary, huge demon standing before her. She stood up with courage and pushed the demon out of the cave. She went straight to the wise sage living in the village.

The sage told, "He is a powerful demon Sambasadhana. It seems as if Lord Shiva himself has given him the power to destroy everything in this universe. As far as I know, no one has the power to destroy him except the monkey leader Kesari. I do not know where he may be at this moment and how to convince him to help you."

Suddenly Sambasadhana broke the shackles. Something hit him so hard that the demon became deaf. The demon fell down due to unbearable pain. The sage turned back and saw a strong monkey standing with his hands on his hips and a smile on his face. The sage said in surprise, "Kesari." Anjana opened her eyes. Kesari was standing there.

Sambasadhana regained his composure and pounced on Kesari. Kesari's strength was formidable. Both of them exchanged blows on each other's bodies. The entire village including all the sages and saints gathered to watch the fight. Sambasadhana transformed into a huge elephant. He started demolishing everything that came in his reach. Not a single house was left standing. Kesari was also not aware of anything due to the fear of the villagers and sages and saints.

The very next moment Kesari made himself small. He climbed on the elephant and started hitting his forehead with his tightly clenched fist. Even though Kesari had shrunk in stature, his blows were powerful. The head of an elephant is its weakest part. Kesari knew this and so he kept punching the elephant's head. Sambadhana was bleeding. He did not die. He ran away shaking his head. Finally Kesari killed Sambadhana.

The sages and villagers jumped with joy hailing their savior Kesari. They lifted him on their shoulders. Tears rolled down Anjana's eyes. These were tears of joy. The sages proposed Kesari to accept Anjana as his wife.

Both agreed. The sages blessed the happy couple and said, "Through this marriage a historic person will be born who will create a revolution in the world of devotion. His glory will be so intense that all the three worlds will tremble seeing his power." Thus Hanuman was born.

There is another story related to Hanuman. Rama returned to Ayodhya after conquering Lanka. The aged Hanuman was meditating on the shore of the same sea which was witness to his many adventures with Rama. Suddenly someone pushed Hanuman. Hanuman opened his eyes and saw a black figure inciting him for a fight. The black figure started teasing him. He called him a foolish monkey. This was Kali Yuga, his age. Shani started pushing Hanuman with great force. Shani was flying in the air holding Hanuman's tail tightly. Hanuman got angry and took Shani straight into the sea. He started thrashing him on the rocks of the sea with great force. Shani got injured.

Shani said arrogantly, "Hanuman! You may be physically powerful, but mentally I am much more powerful than you. You could not defeat me in mental games."

Hanuman told Shani, "I am not an ordinary human being. I was counted among the divine people."

Shani replied, "This is not possible. Anyone who lives in this world lives under my jurisdiction." Teasing Hanuman, Shani further said, "My favorite targets are old people who are close to death."

Hanuman said, "Alright. Show me how you affect people's minds?"

On hearing this, Shani immediately jumped on Hanuman's head. Due to which he started having severe headaches. Hanuman picked up the mountain and placed it on his head. Hanuman did not feel its weight on his head. Inside Hanuman's head, Shani was feeling the full weight of the mountain on his back. Hanuman's headache did not reduce. Hanuman picked up the second mountain and placed it on top of the first mountain. The pressure on Shani's back increased rapidly. Shani started screaming loudly. Hanuman placed third and then fourth. As soon as Hanuman tried to place the fifth mountain on his head, Shani started screaming loudly.

Shani groaned in pain and said, "O Hanuman! Let me go. I beg of you."

Hanuman, feigning surprise, said, "Promise me that you will not stay in my body for so long."

He proceeded to lift the fifth mountain. Shani became angry. Then calming down, Shani declared, "I will not even think of entering Hanuman's house. Not only this, I will not trouble anyone who chants your name."

Hanuman dropped all the mountains one by one. Shani flew off Hanuman's head and fell to the ground writhing in extreme pain.

Writhing in pain, Shani requested Hanuman, "Every part of my body is aching. Massage me with oil."

Hanuman said, "I am an ascetic. I do not have oil." Hanuman advised Shani, "You should ask for oil from those people whom you trouble."

It is said that from that day onwards, every person coming to the Shani temple offers a little oil to soothe his pain.

❐

***Bhoot Pisaach Nikat Nahin Aavai |***
***Mahavir Jab Naam Sunavai || 24***

[If one chants the name of Mahavir, ghosts and demons do not come near.]

## The Essence

A new demon named Trayambakasura was enhancing his powers. On hearing this, everyone was worried. Hanuman also saw that four divine looking people were worshipping the earth with special mantras. All of them were deities in charge of Dharma, Artha, Kama and Moksha. The earth cracked. Before they could jump into the pit, he stopped them just in time. When they were asked for an explanation, they said, "There is no point in living on planet Earth. Trayambakasura demon is occupying all parts of the universe. A great evil is about to happen." They explained to Hanuman that the body of this demon is so huge that it is overpowering even him. He has received a boon from Shiva. Trayambakasura asked for the boon of living forever, but Shiva refused to give this boon. He got one boon after another.

First of all, he asked Brahma about the characteristics of the land. He asked Shiva to grant him a boon that he would never be killed by any weapon or by anyone who was under the care of Lord Shiva. Then he turned to the preserver of the entire universe. He asked him for the sight to see both visible and invisible objects. Vishnu gave him the ability to see anyone anywhere.

Now Trayambakasura declared war against the gods in heaven. Then those four divine-looking people fled. Trayambakasura ordered his minister, "Go! Capture all four and bring them here."

On hearing Trayambakasura's order, the minister ran to capture them but unfortunately Hanuman came in between. Hanuman struck the minister with his mace. He fell far away. Hanuman hid all four in trees. Hanuman hid Dharma inside golden leaves in a banyan tree, Kama inside a Kadamba tree, Moksha inside a Peepal tree and Artha inside a golden leaf tree. Hanuman called Jambavan to protect the four purusharthas hidden inside the trees and Hanuman left for heaven to deal with the demon Trayambakasura.

Trayambakasura had assumed the form of a god. A strange situation had arisen in heaven.

But the duplicate form had the same strength as the original but not intelligence. All the gods were fighting with their own duplicate forms.

Trayambakasura's minister, who was beaten by Hanuman, returned with a damaged face. That minister told Trayambakasura how he failed to capture the four purusharthas due to the cleverness of a monkey. The immediate destruction of the four purusharthas was necessary. As soon as they are destroyed, the gods can be destroyed. Trayambakasura thought about how to destroy the four purusharthas? Using the power given by Vishnu, Trayambakasura found out that Hanuman had hidden the four in the forest. Hanuman reached there before Trayambakasura could reach there. He came and stood between them. Trayambakasura made a replica of Hanuman. But this replica was black in colour and had the same strength.

The battle between the two Hanumans began, creating tremendous vibrations. Tridev appeared to control the situation.

The dark-coloured Hanuman did not have the intelligence of the real Hanuman. Tridev also got confused. The real Hanuman used his intelligence and made another replica of himself, exactly like the fake black Hanuman of Trayambakasura. After this, both the dark-coloured Hanumans merged into one and immediately assumed the form of a deity. The three major gods blessed the dark-coloured Hanuman that he would be worshipped in this form. When the souls troubled by ghosts, spirits and evil powers worship the dark-coloured Hanuman, they immediately get relief from all such troubles.

Hanuman returned to the gods who were still afraid of the demon. There was a cow named Surabhi in heaven. The cow Surabhi accepted Hanuman's request and gave place to the three gods in her body.

Hanuman requested Jambavan to get the four Purusharthas there too. At the same time. Trayambakasura reached there and challenged Jambavan. The battle went on for long. Jambavan used Brahmapasha to bind the demon. The battle ended. Jambavan took the four Purusharthas to the place where Hanuman and Surabhi were waiting.

Hanuman hid the Surabhi cow in the ashram of Matang Rishi. Trayambakasura understood the trick and kidnapped the cow. He took the Surabhi cow to Pataal Lok. His plan was to perform Gomedha Yagna. In this yagna, the cow is sacrificed. Just before the yagna was to be completed, Hanuman appeared and blew away everything by creating a tornado. He destroyed the whole yagna area. Trayambakasura got angry at Hanuman. He ran to kill Hanuman. Before the battle could start between Hanuman and Trayambakasura, Surabhi came between them. Hanuman planned to kill the demon through Surabhi instead of any weapon. Surabhi was innocent and weaponless. The Surabhi cow continued to attack the demon using her horns until he breathed his last.

Then the gods appeared from Surabhi. They declared that since she had protected them like a mother she would always be worshiped as a mother throughout the world. They blessed Hanuman for not giving up till the end and thus saving the world.

❐

***Nasai Rog Harai Sab Peera |***
***Japat Nirantar Hanumat Bira || 25***

[By constant chanting of the name of heroic Hanuman, all diseases are cured and all pains are removed.]

## The Essence

Ravana happily started talking to himself, "It will be a lot of fun to take revenge from the powerful monkey clan. I have polluted the water of the rivers of Sumeru by deploying the five-hooded snake Panchfan. Life is not possible without water. No one can accuse Ravana of poisoning the rivers. Hey! My name is Dashagriva. I am Dashanan. Why should I make such a mistake that the world points a finger at me? The only thing is that the people who drink the water of these rivers will become mentally weak. Then he will become Ravana's slave. Hey, I will hypnotize all of them and bring them under my control. I know that bodily functions are controlled by the five winds. These are: Prana, Apana, Vyana, Samana and Udana. They control breathing, digestion, excretion and so on. What else do I need? I will become more powerful by controlling the body and mind of the monkeys."

King Kesari was aware that their water was being contaminated but he had no idea who was behind it. He started digging wells to overcome the water shortage. Hanuman soon dug hundreds of wells in the entire kingdom by using his tail. Ravana had not even imagined that his best plan would fail. The plan failed and Kesari got the information about the top secret plan made by Ravana.

As soon as Hanuman came to know about this long-term plan of Ravana, he did not limit his action plan to just digging the well. He started working on a plan beyond this. He decided to punish Panchaphan. Panchaphan ran away. The next night Panchaphan came inside silently again and bit Kesari. Hanuman got angry and caught the Panchaphan snake. He took out the precious gems from the top of its hood. The gems on the hood of the snake are considered to be its highest glory, pride and arrogance. Hanuman broke that pride.

As soon as Hanuman's hand was on the fifth one, someone stopped him. Panchaphan's fifth gem would have been destroyed and he would have died. Panchaphan's mother pleaded with Hanuman, "O Hanuman! Please leave my son. I promise you that if you let him go, he will never trouble any living creature. Please have mercy on my son with your big heart."

On hearing a mother's cry, Hanuman loosened his grip. Panchaphan slid out. Panchaphan humbly told Hanuman- "I will fulfill my mother's words." Then he fell at Hanuman's feet and said, "O son of wind! Forgive me. Give me a place at your feet. Hanuman forgave him. Panchaphan became a devotee of Hanuman.

Panchaphan felt remorseful about his mistake. He folded his hands and humbly requested Hanuman, "I have done a despicable act by biting your father and your relatives. This will have disastrous consequences. If we don't treat them within two days, they will die." Saying this, tears started flowing from Panchaphan's eyes. He suggested, "We can ask Shukracharya, the guru of all demons, to give us his Sanjivani mantra which has the healing powers to bring everyone back to life."

Panchaphan knew Shukracharya closely. He willingly went to him and requested. He was disappointed. Panchaphan returned and told Hanuman, "To save your clan, we have to procure a herb called Vaishali Karna Pushp which grows only on the Prabal Dvip. The path to this island is not only dangerous, but this herb is also available only to a select few. Only he who passes the three criteria of being an innocent child, a Brahmachari and a Tridev can enter the Prabal island situated a hundred yojanas away."

Hanuman got ready to go. Panchaphana had already told Hanuman that the red flowers were guarded by a cruel Brahmarakshas. Mayasura came in disguise and guided him. He did not want Hanuman to succeed. So Mayasura sent Hanuman on a wild goose chase. After hours of wandering Hanuman finally reached his destination.

Brahmarakshas was famous for swallowing everything. He was a sage in his other birth. He was cursed to become a Brahmarakshas. The curse would be ineffective only when a divine power enters his mouth. Hanuman entered his mouth. Being a divine power Hanuman killed the demon and freed him from the curse. The sages were so grateful to be freed from the curse that they offered rare flowers to Hanuman. Hanuman returned home. He gave flower medicine to his father and all the sick monkeys. All became conscious and healthy.

Hanuman was going towards Shani's residence to bring him when on the way Hanuman collided with planet Mangal, considered to be the god of war. Wrestling lovers also consider him the god of wrestling. Hanuman overpowered Mangal and proceeded further. He pressed Mangal under his arm and went to find Shani. When he reached near Shani's area, the security guard stopped him. When he removed him from his way, he had a confrontation with Ratna Mai as the next obstacle.

When he removed her and cleared the way, Hanuman came in front of Swarna Mai. Swarna Mai is famous by the name of Sade Sati. After controlling her also, Hanuman reached the innermost area of Shani. He patiently requested Shani to return with him. Shani attacked his head. Both of them clashed. Helpless Shani asked for forgiveness. He agreed to return. Suryadev was very happy to get his son back. Shani asked for forgiveness from his father.

❐

### *Sankat Te Hanumana Chhudavai |*
### *Man Kram Vachan Dhyana Jo Lavai || 26*

[Hanuman frees those from difficulties who meditate on him in thought, deed and word.]

## The Essence

A demon named Sambhasadana was killed by Kesari.

Sambhasadana's brother Kumbhasadan shouted and asked, "Where is Sambhasadana?" He roared at the assembled demons- "Oh! Have you not heard?" They started wailing. "Your brother Sambhasadana is dead. The monkey king Kesari killed him mercilessly." His fellow demons were still mourning his death. They were drained of their energies and motivation like orphans who had no one to take care of them. "I will avenge my brother's death!" Kumbhasadan stumbled and almost fainted groaning in pain.

Meanwhile Anjana was upset and angry with the child Hanuman for his mischief. Complaints of Hanuman's mischief were coming in continuously. All the sages were complaining about Hanuman to mother Anjana. How Hanuman interrupts the meditation of those sages. How he interrupts their rituals. How he played pranks on them? Anjana was very upset with such complaints. Troubled Anjana tied child Hanuman with iron shackles to stop his mischief. Mother thought that by doing this Hanuman's mischief will stop.

On the other hand Kumbhasadan was planning to kill Kesari. Child Hanuman realized that evil forces are plotting against his innocent father. He broke his shackles and reached near Kumbhasadan. Seeing Hanuman suddenly Kumbhasadan fell on the ground. Hanuman didn't let him get up. He also threw other demons away. Kumbhasadan was left alone. Child Hanuman punched him hard. He died.

There was a demon named Guhasur. He would sleep for six months and remain awake for six months. One of his specialties was that when he woke up and breathed loudly, all the insects around him were drawn towards him and he swallowed them all. Guhasur was sleeping peacefully in a cave. No one dared to disturb him.

One day, while playing, Hanuman along with his friends reached near the cave where the demon Guhasur lived. Hanuman asked his friends, "Why do we stay away from that big cave? It seems to be a good place to play."

One friend said, "We can't go there."

"Why can't we go?" Bal Hanuman asked curiously.

All the friends said together, "Because Guhasur is sleeping there!"

The second friend said, "We can be drawn by his breath. So consider that we are 'dead.'"

Telling the previous incident, the third friend said, "He ate many of our friends."

Hanuman said-,"Come with me. I will see what Guhasur can do."

All his friends followed him inside.

Guhasur was asleep. All the birds were jumping and playing on him. When Guhasur was about to wake up, Hanuman planned to kill him before he could take a single breath. Hanuman jumped on Guhasur. Before Guhasur could react, Hanuman jumped on him again. Due to Hanuman's heavy weight, the demon's body started bleeding. He died due to excessive bleeding. All Hanuman's companions started dancing in joy.

Hanuman was not only famous for removing troubles from his devotees in Treta and Dwapar Yuga, but in Kali Yuga his importance was the same as in the earlier times. Mughal emperor Akbar had heard a lot about the specialties of Tulsidas ji. One day Akbar ordered, "Call Saint Tulsidas to the court immediately." He was eager to meet Saint Tulsidas.

Tulsidas came to the Mughal court. Every person in his court stood up after seeing the saint. Akbar was surprised. Akbar said to Tulsidas ji, "I have heard that you have mysterious powers. I want to see what you can do?"

Tulsidas replied, "I do not have any magical powers. I only chant the name of Rama. This is the only magic I have."

Akbar got angry on hearing this. He ordered, "Put him in the dungeon!"

It is said that a large number of monkeys gathered in Akbar's court.

Akbar didn't anticipate that such a large number of monkeys would gather due to Tulsidas ji's chanting of Rama's name. He didn't know how to deal with this calamity? A minister suggested that Tulsidas ji be released from captivity. Akbar freed Tulsidas ji and called him and said, "Save me from these dangerous monkeys."

Tulsidas stopped chanting the name of Rama. The monkeys went away from there. Seeing this, Mughal emperor Akbar was surprised. Then he understood how much power there is in the name of Rama.

❐

### *Sab Par Rama Tapasvi Raja |*
### *Tin Ke Kaj Sakal Tum Saja || 27*

[The ascetic king Lord Rama reigns over all and you have completed all his tasks.]

## The Essence

Nal and Neel had built a bridge over the sea. The monkey army was about to reach Lanka from the bridge when Ravana destroyed both ends of the bridge with two Agneyastra. The monkey army got stuck in the middle of the sea. The situation was such that the monkeys could neither reach Lanka nor return. It was a very difficult situation. Hanuman thought about it and expanded his size. He pulled the ends of the bridge with his hands towards the land of Lanka. The army started landing on the land of Lanka. In this way he didn't let any of Rama's tasks remain incomplete or unsuccessful.

Once such a situation arose in Ayodhya that everyone became completely dissatisfied with Hanuman. Everyone decided to end his services. Sita and Bharat also agreed to this proposal of keeping Hanuman out of the palace. Hanuman was sent out of Ayodhya for a favor.

Sita handed over the list of tasks required for Rama to complete the formality. Rama saw the list and nodded his head. Everyone was happy that at least they will be able to serve Rama without being under Hanuman's shadow.

When Hanuman returned, he found out that Rama's services had been divided and Hanuman's name was not included in the list of sevadars. He was surprised. This list had Rama's approval.

They claimed that one service was not included in the list.

One sevadar asked the other, "What went wrong? Which service was left out from the list?"

The other sevadar said laughingly, "Oh brother! No service was left out from the list. This is some trick of Hanuman. His name is not among the sevadars. That is why he is upset."

The first sevadar took a deep breath and said, "I don't believe it. Hanuman has read the entire list and he is a very old sevadar of Lord Shri Rama. Something or the other must be missing."

"He is not telling what is missing."

"Maybe you are right. There is a solution for this as well. Mother Sita herself should tell Lord Shri Rama about Hanuman's claim and ask Hanuman to prove his claim in front of the entire court."

"Yes! This will be right."

Both sevadars went to Mother Sita and told her the entire incident. Sita also agreed with both of them. All three reached Rama. Hanuman was called in the royal court.

Sita asked Hanuman, "Tell me which service is not listed?"

"Snapping service." Hanuman answered straight-faced.

'Snapping service'? Hearing this, everyone present in the royal court was stunned. What kind of service is this? Everyone was asking each other what kind of service is this?

Sita said in mild anger, "There is no such service. You are saying anything."

With folded hands, Hanuman said politely- "Mother! Whenever Lord Shri Rama yawned, he would snap his fingers. No one was appointed for this extremely important service." No one had any answer. When Rama confirmed Hanuman's statement, there was disappointment in the royal court. Sita was left speechless. Their plan failed.

❐

***Aur Manorath Jo Koi Laavai |***
***Soi Amit Jeevan Phal Paavai || 28***

[Whoever brings their heartfelt wishes you fulfil them with unlimited nectar like fruits.]

## The Essence

When a devotee asked Hanuman, "Should we have wishes or should we be wish less?" Hanuman gave a pleasant reply. He said, "I don't like anyone asking anything from my Lord Rama. So I want no one to ask anything from Lord Rama." So the devotee asked again, "Does this mean that we should not have any wishes?"

Hanuman replied, "No, no! Please have wishes. Because I take the responsibility of fulfilling every wish. It is my vow to fulfill the wish of a devotee so that my lord Rama does not have to worry about it."

Hanuman was in the beautiful Ashok Vatika of Lanka. He was thinking of a way to meet Sita. He was planning on how to break through Ravana's security system. Finally, Hanuman assumed a small form. Slowly he came down before Sita. Sita felt a little uneasy seeing a stranger before her. Hanuman assured Sita that he was Rama's servant. Then Sita and Hanuman talked to each other for a long time. When Hanuman took out the ring given by Rama for Sita, Sita became even more overwhelmed. Tears flowed from her eyes.

Hanuman said to Sita, "O Mother Sita! You sit on my back. I am able to take you out of Lanka."

Sita said to him, "Son! You managed to cross the ocean to reach me which is not an easy task by any means. So definitely you are powerful and intelligent. But I have a doubt. I am confused. What is your real size?"

Hanuman had appeared before Sita in a very small form. Sita could not even imagine how he could take her back? Hanuman said, "I am very small, mother. But with the grace of Lord Rama, I can become very big when needed. God's power is so great that I can even become big by taking refuge in him. But my actual size is small."

Sita was impressed by Hanuman's answer.

This was the last day of Rama's exile. Bharata, his brother Shatrughna, his ministers, the citizens of Ayodhya were all present around him. Bharata had made up his mind to jump into the pyre of fire when Rama was late in coming. Hanuman was sent in advance to inform about Rama's arrival.

It was the miracle of nature or the fate of destiny that some time ago Hanuman was sitting on a tree to save Sita from committing suicide and today he is sitting on a tree to save Bharata's life.

Hanuman started Rama Leela in his sweet voice and narrated the story of Rama reaching Sage Bharadwaj's ashram. Bharata heard this message. Rama has reached near Ayodhya. Awareness and enthusiasm filled Bharata's heart. He gave up the idea of ending his life.

❐

***Charon Jug Partap Tumhara |***
***Hai Parsiddh Jagat Ujiyara || 29***

[Your glory is famous in all the four yugas and your fame illuminates the entire world.]

## The Essence

Hanuman's character is incredible. He has been honoured with the title of Purushottam. He is immortal. It is said that wherever Rama Katha is told, Hanuman Ji is always present there. He is Lord Shri Rama's intimate councilor. Only Hanuman Ji has the right to take us to Rama's feet.

Brilliance, patience, fame, skill, power, humility, policy, effort, valour and wisdom, all these qualities are always present in Hanuman. He is the king of monkeys. Hanuman, who is endowed with many qualities like patience, seriousness, quick wit, good behaviour, bravery, faith, modesty, humility, modesty, etc., has been mentioned in detail by Maharishi Valmiki and Tulsidas. He has the ability to complete all tasks. His achievements are amazing. The works accomplished by him are multifaceted and astonishing.

Many examples of the extreme purity of the character of virtuous Brahmachari Shri Hanuman, the presiding deity of innumerable Akharas of India, are also found in the Ramayana.

In the ancient scriptures, there is mention of seven immortals who have been blessed with eternal life. These are Ashwatthama, Vyas, Kripacharya, Markandeya, Bali, Vibhishan and Hanuman. In the eyes of scholars, Hanuman's achievements are divine.

He is one of the greatest persons in all the ages. The one who takes refuge in him becomes free from all troubles.

In the Ramayana written by Maharishi Valmiki, through many stories, Hanuman's character traits are revealed, which highlight his fame in the world.

❐

***Sadhu Sant Ke Tum Rakhware |***
***Asur Nikandan Ram Dulare || 30***

[You are the protector of saints and sages, destroyer of demons and the favourite of Lord Rama.]

## The Essence

We all know and Tulsidas ji has duly clarified in Hanuman Chalisa that the sages had a special attachment towards Hanuman since his childhood. Child Hanuman would run away pulling the beards of sages, creating obstacles in yagna, jumping on the laps of sages and troubling them as if these were Hanuman's daily routine. This was in his childhood but later Hanuman would never miss any opportunity to protect sages by using his powers at the right time.

Sage Angiras was considered to be one of the best sages of the time. He was included in the group of Sapta Rishis. Once, Sage Angiras felt that his body was burning like fire. He could not understand the reason for this mysterious heat. He went to Goddess Lakshmi. Lakshmi ji said, "Sage Angiras, the reason for your body burning is the sin you have committed."

"What sin have I committed?" she asked him.

"You have done injustice to Shukracharya by being partial towards your son Brihaspati."

Angiras had appointed his son Brihaspati as the Guru of the Gods by ignoring Shukracharya. Shukracharya vowed to take revenge. He appointed himself as the Guru of the demons.

Sage Angiras asked the Goddess for a solution. Then Goddess Lakshmi said, "Go to Hanuman. Listen to the story of Ashta Siddhis from him. By listening to this, your sins will gradually reduce and you will soon get well."

Sage Angiras went to meet Hanuman. Hanuman was very happy. Hanuman was going somewhere so he asked the sage to accompany him and narrated a story on the way. As the story progressed, the fierce fire in the sage's stomach started reducing. Thus, due to Hanuman, sage Angiras became healthy once again.

Hanuman became famous by many names like Shankar Suvan, Kesari Nandan and Pawan Tanay. After Hanuman returned from Lanka, Rama called Hanuman his son. This was Hanuman's new identity. Rama said to Hanuman, "Every son on earth is indebted to his parents. But on this earth you are the only son whose father is indebted to you."

❐

***Ashtasiddhi Nau Nidhi Ke Data |***
***As Var Deen Janki Mata || 31***

[You are the giver of eight mystical powers and nine types of wealth, as blessed by Mother Sita.]

## The Essence

Many types of siddhis (mystical and supernatural powers) are mentioned in our ancient Vedic literature. Out of these, eight siddhis are considered important. These eight siddhis are called Ashta Siddhi. Hanuman Ji has eight mystical powers. These are as follows:

### 1. Anima

The ability to shrink his body to the size of an atom as per requirement.

### 2. Mahima

The ability to expand the body to any size.

### 3. Garima

The ability to make the body extremely powerful and heavy.

### 4. Laghima

The ability to make the body light.

### 5. Prapti

The ability to go to any place without any obstruction.

### 6. Prakamya

The ability to fulfill any desire.

### 7. Isitva

The ability to have complete authority over anything and everything

### 8. Vasitva

The ability to manipulate every living being

Hanuman, the lord of the eight siddhis, is also the lord of the nine nidhis. Nidhi generally means wealth. After Kubera, if there is any god of wealth, it is Hanuman. According to ancient scriptures, each nidhi has been personified as a goddess.

### Hanuman has nine nidhis -

**1. Mahapadma**

The great lotus flower

**2. Padma**

Lotus or a lake situated in the Himalayas

**3. Shankh**

Conch

**4. Makara**

Crocodile

**5. Kachhapa**

Tortoise or turtle shell

**6. Mukunda**

Cinnabar

**7. Kunda**

Jasmine

**8. Nila**

Sapphire

**9. Kharva**

Dwarf

According to this quatrain, Sita blessed him with 8 siddhis and 9 nidhis. Siddhis refer to supernatural and mystical powers attained through yoga and meditation.

Hanuman received 14 boons from Brahma, Indra and other gods in his entire life. Over the period of time, while serving Rama and Sita, Hanuman received 21 more boons. These boons made Hanuman a prosperous being.

On hearing a soft voice of "Help, help!" Hanuman ran towards the voice for help. He saw a little girl jumping out of a deep ditch in the forest on a mountain. Hanuman pulled the girl out of the ditch.

"What are you doing here?" Hanuman asked in surprise.

"My stepmother has sent me to collect wood for cooking. If I am late, the food will be delayed. Then my stepsisters will beat me badly. I have to go. Thank you for saving me." Saying this, the girl left.

Hanuman got curious. He followed Mamta. Hanuman saw that her stepmother and stepsisters beat her badly for coming home late. Hanuman made a plan to teach the evil family a lesson or two. As per the plan, Hanuman disguised himself as a beauty doctor and went to that family. The stepsisters wanted to become the most beautiful girls so that they could marry a prince. Hanuman gave the stepsisters herbs to apply on their faces and said, "After applying these herbs on your faces, do not think ill of anyone. If you do, your face will turn black."

In their excitement to become beautiful, the stepsisters did not pay heed to the warning of Hanuman who was disguised as a doctor. They had only negative and hateful thoughts about innocent Mamta. Their faces turned black. Hearing their evil words, Mamta started crying helplessly. Hanuman pacified Mamta. While preaching to the evil family, Hanuman said, "It is not Mamta's fault that you have become black. By misbehaving with her and always thinking the worst for her. The beauty of the heart is more important than the outer beauty."

Hanuman looked at Mamta and said, "Don't worry Mamta. I am here, your brother. I will always protect you."

With Hanuman's blessings, Mamta got married to a prince.

Kashyap Nidhi is the rarest of the Nidhi. It is considered a symbol of wealth and prosperity. At that time it was only with Indra. Indra came to know that Hanuman has set out in search of Kashyap Nidhi. Indra did not want Hanuman to get Kashyap. He decided to put obstacles in Hanuman's path. Kashyap Nidhi was in Kashyap Lok, an ocean full of turtles. There was Kashyap, the king of turtles. The king said to Hanuman, "To get Kashyap Nidhi, you will have to go through very difficult tasks. This is a difficult task. You should give up this idea."

Hanuman replied, "I am here on the orders of my guru Suryadev. Let me tell you that I will never accept defeat."

The king was pleased and said, "Tell me what three qualities are necessary to protect wealth?"

Hanuman replied, "To protect wealth, first of all the person who is protecting it should be powerful. Secondly, one should know how to use wealth properly and thirdly, with whom the wealth is worth sharing."

King Kashyap agreed with Hanuman and said, "I will test you on these three parameters. If you succeed in all three, only then will I give you the Kashyap Nidhi."

Hanuman had to fight a giant tortoise to demonstrate his power. Hanuman fought a fierce battle with the extremely huge tortoise. In the middle, the tortoise stopped the fight and said to King Kashyap, "I accept defeat because Hanuman has fought with great love and compassion. He is worthy of Kashyap Nidhi."

Next test: Is Hanuman a good judge of using wealth? He was given some wealth to spend on earth. Hanuman met a woman who was in a bad condition. But Hanuman refused to help her. She said that there were many people around her who were trying to snatch her wealth. Going further Hanuman saw a man beating her children for eating food. He ignored that too because no one appreciates what comes easily. Then Hanuman's eyes fell on a businessman. He was about to go bankrupt. That businessman was having food. Some poor children came to him asking for food, so he happily gave his plate to them. Hanuman thought that this is a good candidate to give money because he can help more people by being a fair employer and he will not hesitate to give charity also.

So, Hanuman gave some part of his wealth to that businessman. Now Indra created a scene where he disguised himself as a money lender and beat some people for not returning the loan. Hanuman was seriously disturbed. Hanuman decided to give those people some money to repay their debt. They spent it on their pleasures. Just then King Kashyap appeared. He informed Hanuman that he had failed the test. Hanuman justified that if he had not given him the money the money lender would have killed him. In this case he valued life more than money. Satisfied with his answer, King Kashyap passed him and took him for the next test of consciousness.

He asked Hanuman to enter a kingdom from the north. It was a kingdom built by King Kashyapa specifically for this test. The law was that whoever enters the kingdom from the northern gate after the king dies will be crowned as the new king. Hanuman entered from the north so he was garlanded and declared the king. He was surprised by this foolish method of finding a new king. He was not interested in power but in making sensible rules for the future. Hanuman travelled all over the kingdom to make the right person the king. He saw a farmer ploughing his land without the help of an ox. Hanuman spoke to the farmer and found out that since he didn't want to trouble his oxen, he was ploughing himself. Hanuman was pleased to know that the farmer was concerned about the welfare of the animals.

He then asked for water. The farmer took him to his house and offered him food along with water. Hanuman saw simple food on the plate and asked if he ate this simple food every day. The farmer replied that he believed in simple living and high thinking. Instead of the satisfaction of delicious food, he preferred the satisfaction of helping people. Hanuman asked him about his family, to which the farmer replied that the whole kingdom was his family and he provided them with food by farming. Hanuman was pleased that he had found the right person to crown him as the king. But he also wanted to assess how powerful he was because a king must have physical strength.

Just then some people came to attack the farmer with sticks. They had to settle old scores with him. The farmer, who was fearless, fought alone. He picked up a strong stick and wielded it with such agility that all the thugs started running to save their lives. Finding an opportunity, Indra also came in disguise to fight the farmer. The poor farmer was no match for him. Hanuman saw that it was Indra who was trying to foil his plans. He immediately transferred some of his power to the farmer and soon the farmer overcame the last challenge as well.

Hanuman, on royal command, declared that the farmer was fit in every way to become the king of the land. King Kashap was pleased to see Hanuman victorious in all his trials and handed over the Kashap Nidhi to him. Kashap Nidhi himself was very happy to be with Hanuman, he was confident that Hanuman would use the divine wealth only for the welfare and well-being of all living beings.

After the battle, Rama sent Hanuman to inform Mata Sita of Rama's victory over Ravana. Hearing this wonderful news, Sita's heart overflowed with blessings for Hanuman. "May all worthy virtues reside in your heart; May the Lord of skill always be kind to you. Because this day is very auspicious, it will be known as Mangalvaar (Tuesday) and you will be worshipped on this day. May you be blessed with the eight siddhis and nine nidhis." *As bar dinha Janaki Mata.*

❐

***Rama Rasayan Tumhare Pasa |***
***Sada Raho Raghupati Ke Dasa || 32***

[You have the treasure of the holy name of Rama and you should always remain in the service of Rama.]

## The Essence

O Hanuman! You have the nectar of devotion to Lord Rama. You will always remain his loyal servant. Lord Shri Ram himself became indebted to you. Rama said, "O Hanuman! You have saved the entire Raghuvansh, the mighty Lakshman and me too in a righteous manner today by finding out about Videhrajanandini Sita, meeting her and giving her good news,"

On another occasion, Rama had said, "O Hanuman! I am ready to sacrifice my life to repay the debt of each of your favors, but if many of your favors remain, then we along with our family will always remain indebted to you. I do not want to become indebted to you. I wish that your favors get digested because someone is repaid only when he is in trouble. Even in my dreams, I do not want that any trouble ever comes to you."

On the occasion of Rama's coronation, Hanuman found the necklace and started looking for the name of Rama in it. This story is well known.

Hanuman wanted to know the details of the whole story due to which he received death threats. The King of Kashi explained. He said, "The person who had vowed to kill him by sunset was none other than Lord Rama."

Hanuman was in a dilemma. On one hand he had vowed to his mother to save the king and on the other hand he had loyalty towards Lord Rama. For the first time in his life he was in a situation where he had to stand against Rama. He regretted surrendering to his mother even before understanding the whole problem. If only his mother had known this, she would not have even recommended this mission if Hanuman had to stand against Rama. Hanuman had to find a solution anyhow. The only solution he had was the holy name of Lord Rama and he believed that this was the solution to all the problems of life.

Hanuman suggested to the King of Kashi "that he should stand neck deep in the water of the Sarayu River and continuously chant the name of Lord Rama." As per Hanuman's instructions, the King of Kashi started chanting Lord Rama's name. After some time, the intensity of the King's chanting increased. By sunset, he was chanting Lord Rama's name loudly. Just at sunset, Rama shot an arrow to behead the King of Kashi. The King of Kashi began to sense his approaching death. The intensity of his chanting of Rama's name increased. The arrow was caught by Hanuman's powerful hand an inch before it entered the King's throat. Hanuman snatched the arrow and broke it into two pieces and threw it into the river. The King of Kashi took a deep breath.

Rama shot a second arrow. Hanuman caught the arrow again. The third arrow had the same fate. The King was thrilled that all three of his arrows had gone out. He was still alive. He started dancing in the water in great joy, thanking Hanuman profusely. A huge crowd gathered on the river bank. Rama himself stood with his hands on his hips. Rama was furious at Hanuman for failing three attempts. Rama said to Hanuman, "How dare you stop the arrows of your master? Has your loyalty changed?

Hanuman said with great humility, "I wanted to make everyone assembled here understand that it is their duty to save a devotee of Lord Rama and especially one who chants his name. The King of Kashi was repeating the name of Rama. It was my utmost duty to save his life. Even if the danger came from Lord Rama himself."

Rama could not refute this argument. Hanuman quietly signaled the King to bow to Sage Vishwamitra. The King immediately fell at the feet of the Maharshi and apologized for the disrespect. The Sage forgave him immediately. The King was very grateful to Hanuman.

❒

***Tumhare Bhajan Rama Ko Pavai |***
***Janam Janam Ke Dukh Bisravai || 33***

[By worshipping you, a man can reach Lord Rama and be freed from the sufferings of many births.]

## The Essence

Shri Hanuman Ji is an ardent devotee of Lord Shri Rama. He tore open his chest to show that Shri Rama resides in his heart. He is the leader in achieving the favourite status of Lord Shri Ram due to his ability to cross the ocean as a game and never being arrogant even after doing it. Not because of these qualities, Shri Hanuman Ji has taught his followers that 'If you want to be the favourite of Lord Shri Ram, then serve the Lord without any pride and with this feeling. This will not only fulfill your desire. You will prove the truth of this saying by becoming immortal with the glory of God.

Hanuman got the special joy of freedom in Ayodhya. He had won the heart of every citizen of Ayodhya. No one ever stopped him from entering the royal house. That is why when one day he started following Sita everywhere, no one questioned him and neither did Sita have any objection to this. He was like an innocent son.

Ram loved Sita very much. Hanuman could not understand why Rama loved Sita so much? Sita must have some secret in her mind, because of which Rama loved her so much. If he could uncover Sita's secret, then he too could be as dear to Rama as she was. Hanuman decided that he would keep Mata Sita under constant surveillance throughout the day and surely, he would find out the secret.

Sita observed Hanuman's strange behaviour throughout the day. She realised that he was up to something. Whatever he did was always to please Rama. The way he acted was not always conventional or even the most acceptable. But she tolerated his obvious peeping, constantly observing him. In the evening Sita sat in front of a large mirror and started dressing up. Hanuman stood at a distance and watched Sita getting decked up. Sita took a pinch of red sindoor (vermilion) and applied it on her forehead, rubbing it lightly through her hair. Hanuman found this strange. To clear his doubts Hanuman asked Sita- "O Mother. What have you just done?"

Sita didn't know how to explain to Hanuman the deeper meaning behind the ritual of applying red sindoor. Hanuman was a celibate. He had no experience of the nuances of married life. Sita explained to Hanuman, "This small dot on her forehead made Lord Rama very happy and also ensured a long life for him."

Hanuman had discovered Sita's secret. Hanuman asked the shopkeeper for the red sindoor that Sita had applied on her forehead. The shopkeeper gave a small box containing red sindoor. Hanuman asked for more and the shopkeeper gave him four small boxes full of red sindoor and said, "Even if Sita Mata applies it three times a day, it will not finish even after at least six months."

Hanuman asked him, "Where have you kept the red sindoor powder?"

The unknown shopkeeper pointed inside the shop. Hanuman went into the store room. He went out with a big sack on his shoulder. Hanuman spread all the red sindoor powder from that sack right in the middle of the road. By then many spectators had gathered to see Hanuman's humorous antics. He started rolling on the red sindoor powder and turned red. He arrived in the royal court. Everyone started laughing after seeing him.

However, Hanuman felt satisfied after seeing that Rama also laughed. Rama asked Hanuman, "What did you do? Why did the whole body turn red?"

Hanuman said, "A small red dot on the forehead of Mother Sita can make you happy and increase your age a lot. How happy you will be if I cover myself completely from top to bottom in vermilion. Your age will increase manifold."

Rama blessed Hanuman and said, "Whoever worships you with red vermilion will never have difficulties and sufferings in his life."

If one worships Hanuman, he gets Rams and also ends innumerable sorrows. Hanuman always answers the calls of his devotees and fulfills their prayers regardless of time and place.

❐

### *Antkaal Raghuvar Pura Jayee |*
### *Jahan Janam Hari Bhakt Kahai || 34*

[At the end of life, the devotee goes to the abode of Lord Rama and is reborn as a devotee of Hari.]

## The Essence

There was a demon in Lanka named Jambumaali. Ravana used to call him Jambu lovingly. He loved wine. Ravana gifted him a lake of wine and he built a house in the lake itself.

Seeing the destruction of Ashok Vatika, Ravana ordered all the warriors to reach Ashok Vatika immediately. Jambumali was taken out of the lake by the soldiers. He got agitated. He calmed down when the soldiers told him Ravana's emergency order. He was brought to Ravana. Ravana said to Jambumali, "A good fight awaits you."

Jambumali asked, "Who is my opponent? Is he Indra or Agni?"

"No. He is a monkey." Ravana said.

Jambumali broke the wine glass in his hand and said in anger, "Is this a joke? I do not fight with small monkeys." Then Ravana told him, "This monkey is not a small one. You do not know what he is capable of. He has destroyed the entire Ashok Vatika. He has killed many strong soldiers who were deployed there. He is not an ordinary monkey. Do you understand Jambumali?"

Jambumali said reluctantly, "Hmm! Extraordinary monkey! I will come after finishing him in a while. How much time will it take me to finish one monkey?"

He reached Ashok Vatika. He saw a huge monkey sitting on a dome. He was feasting on fruits. Jambumali was surprised to see this. Hanuman challenged Jambumali on seeing him, "Who wants to meet death today? Come, I will introduce you to death."

Jambumali was angry. He replied to Hanuman, "If you think yourself to be more powerful, then come down. Fight with me. I have seen many monkeys like you." Saying this, he shot arrows at Hanuman. Hanuman caught the arrows and sent them back to Jambumali. Jambumali stopped physical combat and adopted his elusive tactics. He increased his size to even that of Hanuman. Hanuman's size increased by four times. Jambumali was now only up to Hanuman's knees.

Hanuman was willing to fight on equal terms. He said, "Listen Jambu! If you want, I can teach you a small mantra that can save your life. It will destroy all your sins that you have accumulated over many births. If you insist on dying, then chant this mantra."

"What nonsense." Jambu shouted in a frenzy. "A monkey will teach me mantras?"

Seeing his reluctance, Hanuman picked him up and swung him around, balancing him on one finger. All the while he kept saying Rama-ma, Rama-ma. Jambumali was shouting and Hanuman kept swirling at him. Finally, Hanuman threw him away. He died instantly.

❐

***Aur Devta Chitt Na Dharahin |***
***Hanumat Sei Sarva Sukh Karahin || 35***

[All happiness can be achieved by worshipping Hanuman even if one doesn't worship any other gods.]

## The Essence

Rama defeated Ravana and declared the end of the war and ordered Hanuman, "Hanuman! Go quickly and inform Goddess Sita sitting in Ashok Vatika that we have conquered Lanka by granting salvation to Ravana and fulfilling his last wish.

On hearing the extremely auspicious news, Sita said to Hanuman, "May you be blessed, son Hanuman! This auspicious news has filled my heart with joy. I bless you that in Kaliyug, the day of your worship will be called Mangalvar."

Once upon a time, Shukracharya, the guru of demons, said to the demon king named Viprachit, "King! You should organize a Tamasik Yagna."

Viprachit humbly said, "O great Guru! Tamasik Yagna is a negative fire yagna. It creates a high amount of inauspiciousness. Will it be proper to conduct this?"

Shukracharya said, "Performing a yajna will trouble the sages. It will force them to perform a tamasic yajna using disgusting materials like meat and blood."

Shukracharya knew the science of yagnas and was well aware of the fact that the offerings of any yajna had to be accepted by the gods personally. Tamasic yagnas were started with the permission of Viprachit. All the gods started falling sick one after the other.

Surya Dev himself was so sick that the speed of the sun cycle slowed down a lot, resulting in widespread climatic changes all over the world. The rising and setting of the sun also became irregular. Since the sun cycle was disturbed, every living creature on earth naturally got disturbed and started falling sick. Various types of infections and diseases spread all over the world.

When Hanuman came to know that Shukracharya was behind all this, he approached his Guru and guide Surya Dev. Hanuman saw his Guru in that pitiable sick condition. Surya urged Hanuman, "Dear Hanuman! You should stop the evil yagna of Shukracharya by any means and save the universe from an unprecedented disaster."

Surya gave information about the demon king Viprachit and also told where the Gods and sages were kept captive.

Hanuman reached the prison where the sages were kept captive. He came to know from them that they were conducting the yagna not out of their own will but out of compulsion. The demon king had imprisoned all their relatives and threatened to kill them one by one if they did not obey him while performing the Tamasik Yagna. Not only the sages and saints but also their relatives were put in prison.

The prison was created by powerful mantras. It was not easy to penetrate it. Hanuman first decided to root out the fear of the sages. The king and Shukracharya were busy in the Tamasik Yagna and Hanuman was busy in freeing the relatives of the sages from captivity on the top of the mountain. Hanuman sat outside the prison and broke the prison by reciting the name of Rama. All the prisoners were released.

Shukracharya knew through his mystical powers that the spell was broken and he sent the demon army to handle the situation. Hanuman was waiting to receive the army. Hanuman killed each and every demon with his powerful mace.

Hanuman instructed the sages to stop performing the Tamasik Yagya. Shukracharya and the demon king were furious at his impudence. The demon king attacked Hanuman. Hanuman assumed such a huge form that Viprachit retreated in fear. Hanuman was about to kill Viprachit when Shukracharya came forward to protect his disciple. Leaving Viprachit with a warning, Hanuman freed all the sages and requested them to start performing regular Yagya to restore the balance that had tilted towards gross negativity. Shukracharya helplessly watched Hanuman disrupt the Tamasik Yagya and the entire arena collapse before his eyes.

Even after the Tamasik Yagya was stopped, the gods did not recover. Hanuman took them to Dhanvantri for treatment. Dhanvantri tested them and told Hanuman, "Only a special quality of pearl found in Manasarovar can cure them. Apart from this he also needs a twig from the Navratna tree which is a combination of nine different trees growing together."

Hanuman left for Manasarovar to get the ingredients needed for the magical potion to cure the sick gods.

Meanwhile Shukracharya continued the war. He created fake pearls with his yogic powers. These pearls looked like real ones. Hanuman tricked Shukracharya and found the real pearls with the help of the divine swans of Manasarovar. Bringing back the pearls with the sticks of the Navratna tree, Hanuman made sure to complete the yagna as per Dhanvantri's instruction. And much to the delight of all the gods, they all became healthy again.

Hanuman asked Dhanvantri for a permanent cure to all health problems. Dhanvantri told him, "There is a solution. That is Swasthya Nidhi. The problem is that this treasure does not exist. It can only be made by Lord Brahma."

Hanuman reached Brahmlok along with the Gods. Brahma said, "For this, 16 different types of Rudrakshas made from Lord Shiva's tears are needed."

Brahma said to Hanuman, "A Maha Yagya has to be performed with these 16 Rudrakshas."

Hanuman got excited with the idea of performing Maha Yagya and set out to collect 16 materials from holy places. Shukracharya came to know that the Gods were going to perform Maha Yagya. He ordered, "Viprachit! Now you have to foil the Maha Yagya of the Gods. Make arrangements for it."

Viprachit met the king of owls without delay and requested him, "O King! Destroy all the Rudrakshas as soon as possible or else there will be disaster."

When Hanuman could not get the Rudrakshas due to the owls, he became worried. Then he asked Garuda "Who could be behind this mischief? Find out quickly."

Garuda informed Hanuman - "These are the tasks of the owls. Without their permission, no owl can take anything from the king. This is a boon that they have."

Hanuman reached the land of owls. He asked the king to give Rudraksha but the king refused. Hanuman asked the reason,"Why can't you give it? Please give a proper reason."

The king told, "The entire owl family is saddened by the public's perception that we owls are inauspicious. We also want respect in society."

Hanuman expressed sympathy and said, "Don't worry. I will try to end this pain of yours."

Hanuman took the king of owls to Mata Lakshmi. Hanuman requested Lakshmi, "O Lakshmi ji! Find a cure for the pain of this owl community. Find a solution so that they can get respect in human society."

Lakshmi smiled and said, "Such a small thing. From now on owls will not be considered inauspicious. This is my blessing. I will accept them as my vehicle from now on. Now they will be associated with wealth and will be considered auspicious."

The owls gratefully returned the Rudraksha to Hanuman. The Rudraksha was given to Brahma and he started the yagna along with the Gods. Agnidev refused to light up. The reason for this was that Viprachit was controlling the power of the Gods sitting on the throne of heaven. Hanuman reached Indralok in anger and kicked Viprachit from the throne. Viprachit went straight to Pataal Lok and lost all his powers. The Gods regained their powers.

❐

***Sankat Katai Mitai Saba Pira |***
***Jo Sumirai Hanumat Balbira || 36***

[Those who remember the mighty and heroic Hanuman, all their troubles and sufferings are removed.]

## The Essence

Hanuman was going somewhere. He saw some people burning not a human body but a wooden idol. An old woman was screaming loudly nearby. She was wailing continuously about her dead son. A little boy, standing next to her, was trying to console his grandmother by assuring her that his father was not dead. Hanuman wondered why she was conducting the last rites of a living person.

Out of curiosity, he approached the old woman. On Hanuman's asking, the old woman told Hanuman her complicated story, "Her son was alive. While alive, he was like a dead person. Whoever King Baldhari called would never come back."

Hanuman understood that there was some connection between the disappearance of her son and other people and the evil king. Hanuman promised her that he would get to the root of the whole problem and bring her son back.

Hanuman was near the kingdom of King Baldhari. He saw two very weak men about to jump off a cliff to commit suicide. Hanuman stopped them from doing so. He explained compassionately, "Suicide is not the solution to any problem. Problems must be faced with courage."

They were the most powerful wrestlers in the village. One day King Baladhari invited them for a wrestling competition. They accepted the invitation. King Baladhari sucked out all their energy and strength. What was left of them was only a bag of bones while all their powers were transferred to the king."

Hanuman was surprised to hear that. Hanuman thought to himself how did the king get unimaginable power?

Both the wrestlers told Hanuman, "The king had performed penance of Lord Brahma. Lord Brahma was pleased with his penance. He gave a boon to the king that he can draw out the full physical strength of any person standing in front of him. Due to this boon he got the name Baladhari."

The second person told Hanuman "He does not let the person die. If the person dies then his power ends. To maintain his strength he will not let those people die. He will imprison them and feed them well so that they remain alive."

The first wrestler said, "Somehow we both managed to escape from that cave. We were hoping that with our death the king's strength would be reduced and he would be more likely to be defeated."

The two also informed the king about Gajashakti. Hanuman left to meet King Baldhari. The king insulted Hanuman, thinking him to be an ordinary monkey. Hanuman destroyed all the soldiers who came to kill him in a moment. Seeing this Baldhari became serious. Baldhari and Hanuman fought and Hanuman defeated Baldhari easily.

Baldhari tried to snatch Hanuman's energy by holding his hand. Lord Shiva's strength was more than his capacity. Baldhari wanted to let go of Hanuman's hand. Hanuman's energy flowed into his body with a tremendous velocity. When Baladhari's body crossed the extreme point, it split into millions of pieces which scattered all over the place. When Gajashakti regained its strength, Hanuman took him back to his mother. The old mother was very happy and blessed Hanuman a lot.

Sage Narad appeared and requested Hanuman, "Hanuman! You must always take care that in future Baldhari does not exploit the strength of others."

Hanuman promised Narad to fulfil it. He created a beautiful red-coloured deity of himself known as Balnidhi. He told Narada, "This form will always remain in all the arenas and wrestling grounds. Whoever worships this form of mine and performs physical activities and exercises will be able to acquire great strength. Physical activity will keep one strong and lack of it will make one weak."

Narad was very pleased and satisfied to know that there will be no exploitation and suffering now. *Sankat katai mitai sab pira, jo sumirai Hanumat Balbira.* Tulsidas recommended the installation of Hanuman deity in every arena to obtain Hanuman's blessings for strength in wrestling.

❐

***Jai Jai Jai Hanuman Gosain |***
***Kripa Karahun Gurudev Ki Nahin || 37***

[Hail, hail, hail to Lord Hanuman. Please shower your blessings on us as our revered Guru.]

## The Essence

Hanuman was striving to acquire the Ashta Siddhis or the eight mystical powers. He suddenly felt hungry. He looked around but found nothing. Then while performing the Agni Yagna, he saw a weeping ascetic woman. He went to her and saw that the woman's ears were bleeding profusely. Hanuman asked her, "Mother, are you feeling any pain? Please tell me what is troubling you."

"I am performing the Yagna to invoke my death. There is no purpose left in my life," she said crying.

Hanuman asked the woman to tell him everything in detail. The woman said, "After a tough penance, I was blessed with a pair of divine earrings. As per the blessing, I got the power to achieve anything. I can go wherever I want and take any boon from anyone."

Hanuman gasped at the powers she possessed. "Have your earrings been stolen?" he asked sympathetically.

Shaking her head, the woman said, "They were stolen from me by dacoits. ... I am not concerned that they have been stolen. The worry is that they will fall into the wrong hands."

Hanuman set out to find the dacoits. He easily reached them by following the footprints of the horses. On reaching there Hanuman saw that the dacoits were dead. One was about to die. Before dying the dacoit said, "We were bitten by the Nagraja so that he could snatch the earrings from us."

Without delay, Hanuman followed the Nagraja to the sea. Nagraja was situated inside the sea. Hanuman dived deep into the sea and reached the gate of Nagraja. After defeating the guards, he went to meet Nagaraja Kartik. He said to the Nagraja, "Return the precious earrings that you have snatched from dacoits before killing them."

Nagraja refused to do so. Nagraja stung Hanuman. These insignificant stings had no effect on Hanuman because he was the incarnation of Rudra. After defeating the Nagas, Hanuman snatched the earrings. As soon as he picked up the earrings in his hand, all the Nagas became lifeless.

Was there any connection between the two? Hanuman thought. He touched the earrings with the snake to know the connection between the two. The snakes jumped back alive. The earrings belonged to an ascetic woman. Now Hanuman was faced with a tough question: how can it affect the life and death of the snake clan underwater? This was really a surprise for Hanuman.

Nagraja Kartik told Hanuman "These divine earrings are the source of our power. It is really unnatural but unfortunately a few days ago our Naagmani was stolen. When I went to get it back, I found some dacoits who had this pair of earrings. This pair of earrings gave us the same strength as we got from the Naagmani. So I gave up the search for the mani and took these earrings back to Naglok."

Hanuman started thinking that if he took back the earrings then the innocent snakes would die. If he did not do so then the ascetic woman would give up her life. Nagraja folded his hands humbly and said, "We will follow your decision."

Hanuman had to find a third way. He asked Nagaraj- "If I bring back the Naagmani for you, will you return the earrings?"

Nagaraj had no objection to this. Hanuman asked, "Where did you lose the Mani?"

"We had gone to Lord Shiva's abode to participate in the Shivaratri festival. It was stolen from there. Since then we have been lifeless."

"Do you suspect anyone?"

"No, no one."

Hanuman started searching for the Mani on the night of the full moon. The thief was intelligent. He had already hidden the Mani. When Hanuman reached, he did not find a trace of the Mani. Hanuman was confident that the Mani was in the same village. While searching, Hanuman reached a place where a rich man was donating money to the villagers. Hanuman heard from the villagers how this man became rich overnight. Hanuman followed him to his home. Reaching home, he told his servants that he was going hunting to get peace of mind. Hanuman followed him to the forest. The forest was a breeding ground for tigers and the foolish man went all alone. Soon he was attacked by a hungry tiger. Had it not been for Hanuman, he would have lost his life. Hanuman stopped the tiger and took the man in his arms to a safe part of the forest.

The man agreed to hand over the mani to him. He told Hanuman- "Stealing the mani is the biggest mistake of my life. It has only brought me sorrow and misfortune."

Hanuman took the naagmani and returned it to the Nagaraj. The excited Nagaraj returned the divine earrings to Hanuman, who, in turn, handed them over to their rightful owner. The ascetic mother was very pleased with Hanuman.

Hanuman said to the woman, "Please bless me so that I reach Siddhiloka as soon as possible without any obstacles." She not only blessed Hanuman but also gave the earrings. Hanuman was very amazed by that gift and did not know what to do with it.

Woman said in loving words, "You are always ready to help others in distress. Your heart is full of compassion, so you are the rightful owner of the divine earrings."

❑

***Jo Shat Bar Path Kare Koi |***
***Chhutahi Bandi Maha Sukh Hoi || 38***

[Whoever recites this Hanuman Chalisa hundred times will be freed from bondage and experience great happiness.]

## The Essence

Rama returned to Ayodhya after fourteen years of exile. His coronation took place. The sages advised King Rama to perform Ashwamedha to become a Chakravarti emperor. Rama, after consultation with sages, ministers and well-wishers, organized Ashwamedha Yagya. After the yagya, the horse was released. Wherever the horse passed, the rulers of those places accepted Rama's supremacy.

Champak, the son of the king of Surat, stopped the horse. Stopping the horse of Ashwamedha Yagya meant not accepting subordination. That is, war. Whoever wins the horse, gets it. The army followed the horse. Angad was in charge of this army. Angad talked to Champak. Angad was unsuccessful in convincing the king and his son Champak to release the horse. Angad heard from some soldiers of the king of Surat that their king had been blessed with immortality by the god of death.

War was declared. Bharat's son Pushkal was the commander of the first contingent of Rama's army. Champak was a war-experienced warrior. He defeated Pushkal. This time Hanuman went to meet the king after pausing the war for talks.

Hanuman tried to convince the king a lot but he was not ready to listen to anything Hanuman said. Hanuman's spies said that the king was telling his son, “Yamraj had told me that I can leave this body only when Rama himself comes to my residence to free me from the cycle of birth and death. I do not intend to fight a war. I do not intend to trouble my devotees.”

The next day Hanuman came to the battlefield. The king of Surat also appeared on the battlefield to match the strength. Displaying bravery, the king of Surat made Hanuman a prisoner of war.

Hanuman closed his eyes and started chanting the name of Rama. The sky resounded with the holy pronunciation of the word Rama, Rama, Rama. Suddenly the conch started blowing. Rama appeared. Hanuman’s ropes broke. The king of Surat fell on the ground and bowed to Rama. It was a moment of bliss. The king of Surat achieved his desired goal. He attained salvation.

❒

***Jo Yeh Padhe Hanuman Chalisa |***
***Hoye Siddhi Sakhi Gaurisa || 39***

[Anyone who reads this Hanuman Chalisa with devotion will attain siddhi, and Shiva, Lord of Gauri, himself is witness to this.]

## The Essence

After describing all the qualities of Hanuman and the exquisite personality of Rama, Tulsidas ji says that those who regularly chant this Hanuman Chalisa can't be defeated because by reciting it they will get the blessings of both Hanuman and Rama.

Hanuman prevented Queen Satyavati of Kankhal from committing suicide. Hanuman asked Queen Satyavati, "What is lacking in your life? Why did you take the step of jumping into the river?"

"No one can give me what I lack," was her strange reply.

Hanuman asked in surprise, "What do you want?"

"I want a child. I am not able to have a child. I have failed to give the king an heir to continue his legacy. How can I face anyone?" Saying this, the queen burst into tears.

Hearing this, Hanuman met King Narottam and Rajmata of Kankhal. The king said to Hanuman, "I always feel lonely due to not having a child. I feel that my life is aimless."

Consoling him, Hanuman said, "There is a solution to every problem. Some way or the other will definitely be found."

Hanuman meditated on Matang Rishi. Matang Rishi appeared. Hanuman bowed to him and said, "I was helpless to call you. The matter is serious. King Narottam of Kankhal is not having a child. Due to which the kingdom is in trouble. Can you please suggest what can be done in this situation?"

The sage said to Hanuman, "He cannot have a child due to his past sinful deeds."

"Is there no solution, sage?" Is there not a single deed in his past that can save him now? Can he not do anything now? Hanuman asked.

"Yes! Something can be done," said Matang Rishi.

Hanuman asked smilingly, "Tell me the solution, Rishivar."

Sage Matang told, "They should try to please their ancestors."

"I was sure that you will definitely pave some way."

The sage said, "The ancestors will be happy. Then they will be happy to be born in the lineage of the king."

Hanuman was pleased. He thanked the sage and sent him off.

Shukracharya was planning another attack on the gods. He had stopped a powerful demon named Daavanal from his penance. Shukracharya enthusiastically told him his plan.

Shukracharya said to the demon Daavanal, "Daavanal! I want you to go to Pitruloka and capture all the ancestors along with the Aryamanava king. Once they come under our power, we will force them to take birth in demon families."

The demon Daavanal asked in surprise "What will happen by this Acharya?"

Shukracharya explained to him, "In this way the quantitative power of the demons will increase manifold and in this way we will be able to conquer the gods."

"Is this possible? But how will we enter Pitruloka?"

Shukracharya immediately said, "I will give you the power to enter Pitruloka."

Daavanal said smilingly "Alright. If you help, I will prepare my army for the attack."

Here Hanuman was helping King Narottam in Pitru Pooja. At the time of Pind Daan, Hanuman called Goddess Swadha. She had come to accept the donation. Swadha said to Hanuman, "King Narottam's ancestors have got salvation. They are going to a higher planet. None of them will want to come back and take birth on earth again."

Hanuman once again prayed to Matang Rishi for further guidance. Matang Rishi said to Hanuman, "You go to Pitruloka and meet Aryaman and convince the king's ancestors to take birth from Satyavati's womb."

Hanuman followed the instructions and reached Pitruloka. Aryaman revealed, "I am helpless as it is not my or ancestors' decision as to where they will be born. It depends on their past deeds and wishes. Why don't you ask the ancestors where they will be born in the future?"

Ancestors inform Hanuman that they are liberated and cannot accept their wish to be born. One of the Pitris (ancestors) understood Hanuman's wish to save King Narottam and agreed to it.

Hanuman was in Pitruloka when Daavanal started a war against the gods led by Indra. Gods could not counter Daavanal's powers. Daavanal single-handedly conquered all gods and entered Pitruloka. The Pitris hid inside a Peepal tree to escape the horrors of war. Daavanal searched for them everywhere. He heard a message from Shukracharya. The message was to uproot the Peepal tree and bring back all the ancestors.

The Pitris who had willingly agreed to go with Hanuman had already gone with Hanuman and entered Satyavati's womb and impregnated her. The remaining Pitris were taken to the abode of demons where Shukracharya made them motionless by mesmerizing them. Then he performed a yajna so that the Pitris could die and be ready to be born again as demons. He forced Aryaman to instruct the Pitris to take birth in the demon yoni.

Shukracharya boasted, "I will force them to take birth as per my wish."

All the Pitris had died due to Shukracharya's yajna. The result was that Satyavati also gave birth to a dead child. Hanuman approached Shukracharya. He fought with Daanval and killed him and warned Shukracharya to stay away from the affairs of Pitruloka.

After freeing the Pitris, Hanuman consulted the gods. He established a rule that no one can force souls to take birth in any realm or species. The only criteria for taking birth was the activities and desires of the previous life.

After getting a child, Queen Satyavati expressed her gratitude to Hanuman. In the presence of all the gods, she blessed Hanuman that those who glorify Hanuman will be blessed with siddhis.

❐

***Tulsidas Sada Hari Chera |***
***Kijai Naath Hriday Mahn Dera || 40***

[Tulsidas, who is always in the service of Lord Hari i.e. Rama, prays, "O Lord, please reside in my heart."]

## The Essence

It is believed that Tulsidas won the heart of a spirit living on an acacia tree in Kashi. Every morning after bathing, Tulsidas would pour the leftover water at the root of the tree. This water was drunk by the thirsty spirit. One day when Tulsidas was pouring water, he saw a shadow coming out of the tree. He was shocked. He heard a voice, "You have been very kind to me. I will give you a boon. Ask for your heart's desire."

"Who are you?" Tulsidas asked. "And why do you want to give me a boon?"

The voice came, "I am a ghost. I am happy with you. For many years I have not had anything to eat or drink. Ever since I made this tree my home, I have been nourished by the water thrown by you. You have served a pious soul. You have served me well. Now I would also like to serve you."

Tulsidas said, "Give me a boon that I can see Shri Rama."

The ghost laughed happily and said, "If I can give you spiritual boons then why would I be a ghost? Ask for a material boon."

"I have no material desire." Tulsidas replied disappointedly.

The ghost said, "If I don't help you then I will feel ungrateful. So I will share an important thing with you. Listen to me carefully. Every day Rama Katha takes place at Prahlad Ghat in Kashi. You will find a leper there. That leper keeps his face covered with a blanket. He does not know who he is. In reality he is Hanuman, the son of wind. Do not leave him until he promises to take you to Rama."

Upon hearing this, Tulsidas' was stunned. Believing the spirit, Tulsidas reached early to listen to the Rama Katha. He saw a leper already sitting in the last row. The Rama Katha started - and ended. Tulsidas' eyes were only on the leper. When the leper started to leave, Tulsidas ran and caught hold of his feet.

"Please leave me. I am a leper. Don't touch me!" the leper screamed. Tulsidas didn't let him go.

Tulsidas said, "I have recognized who you are. You cannot deceive me. I request you. Take me to your God. I will not leave your feet until then."

Hanuman was impressed by the devotee's intense desire to see God. He knew that Tulsidas was holding Lord Rama's feet instead of his. Hanuman came in his real form. He said, "I cannot assure you of meeting him. I have a suggestion. You go to Chitrakoot and take your time. I will try to bring my master there. He usually does not refuse my request."

Tulsidas followed Hanuman's order. Hanuman gave Tulsidas ji the message of Rama. "Ram will come to meet you not once but twice. You will have to take a test. You will have to recognize Lord Rama yourself."

Tulsidas was very happy to hear the sweet voice from Hanuman's mouth. It was a matter of a few days later. Tulsidas was sitting outside his hut doing some work. Then the Lord and his brother came riding on a horse. Hanuman asked him, "Did you see the Lord?"

Tulsidas said in surprise, "No! Where was he?"

Hanuman told, "Lord Rama has passed by them some time ago riding a horse."

Lamenting, Tulsidas said, "I thought some prince was going for hunting. I made a mistake." Then he fell at Hanuman's feet.

Hanuman consoled him and said, "Rama will come again. This time when Rama comes, I will be with him."

The next time Rama came on the occasion of a festival. Many sages from the surrounding area had gathered to participate in it. Tulsidas wanted to apply sandalwood to all the sages. He kept rubbing sandalwood day and night. Rama came in the form of a child and said, "Baba! Give me some sandalwood."

Tulsidas once again failed to recognize Rama. Hanuman was near Tulsidas ji in the form of a parrot. Sitting on a nearby tree, he started singing,

"*Chitrakoot ke ghat par bhayi santan ki bheed,*

*Tulsidas chandan ghise tilak det Raghuveer.*"

Tulsidas heard this and fell at the feet of the Lord. Finally, he could see his Lord. He was grateful to Hanuman. From that day Tulsidas never stopped singing paeans dedicated to the glories of Hanuman.

❐

# Couplet (doha)

***Pavantanay Sankata Harana Mangala Murati Rupa |***
***Rama Lakhan Sita Sahita Hridaya Basahu Sura Bhupa | |***

[O son of wind-god! Remover of all obstacles, incarnation of auspiciousness, please reside in my heart along with Lord Rama, Lakshman and Sita.]

## The Essence

Tulsidas ji, while expressing gratitude to Hanuman ji, writes that Hanuman is not only a brave man who removes troubles but he is such a unique source of bravery that by just touching him others can also prove their importance by becoming a strong force. He is the son of wind.

Hanuman is the basic mantra of selfless service. His experience, his expression and his work can truly guide society. Even today we hear the echo of the praises of Shri Hanuman ji, who is dedicated to works without any desire and committed to serve for the larger cause.

Even as he is Mahavir (a great warrior), Hanuman is the one who is not proud of his strength even a little. He is the one who is extremely humble, despite being the leader among the wise. He is the one who accomplishes Rama's work, even after scaling the zenith of greatness, being the size of a mountain. He is the one who does not hesitate to make his personality as small as a mosquito for the sake of national work. The ideal character of such a devotee can suppress the demonism of today and take our manhood to Lord.

The entire world is under the control of the five elements, but a devotee who has a strong feeling of dedicating everything for the work of Rama, brings these five elements under his control. Air, sky, earth, fire and water, all these gave timely contribution to Hanumanji. Pawan Dev by blowing forty-nine winds, sky by making the voice of Hanumanji's roar more deep and terrifying, earth by reducing the gravity of the body, fire by protecting Hanumanji, helped him fully in burning Lanka, extinguishing the fire and removing the fatigue.

What is the real form of Hanuman Ji? The first adjective of Hanuman is - *Atulitbaldhama*. Its study shows that Tulsidas ji was not satisfied by just calling Hanumanji strong, rather he wanted to call him something more than strong. This is the reason why he is not called 'Balavan' but 'Baldham' i.e. storehouse of strength.

The second adjective of his body is- *'Hemshailaabhdeham'*. It means that Hanumanji's body is like the aura of a golden rock. This gives the sense that Hanuman, after struggling with difficulties, has become the lord of bright complexion in the same way as gold becomes after being heated in fire. This clearly says that you must toil to succeed amid the hardships..

The third adjective is- *'Danujavanakrishanum'*. Its general meaning is- like fire for the forest of demons. In other words, it can be said as 'Samadrishti' (equal vision). Just like the fire blazing in the forest burns and reduces everyone to ashes without considering the size of the big or small tree, in the same way Hanuman also destroys the demon-like doers.

The fourth adjective is '*Gyaninamagraganyam*', its general meaning is - worthy of being counted first among the wise.

Hanuman is foremost among the wise because he achieved success by removing the troubles like Surasa, Lankini and others from his path by the power of his intelligence and by taking their blessings. He got the good fortune of becoming the eternal companion of Rama.

The fifth adjective is '*Sakalgunanidhanam*'. Its general meaning is - the repository of all virtues. That is, proficient in behaving wickedly with the wicked and behaving genteelly with the gentleman.

The sixth adjective is '*Vanaranaamadhisham*', that is, the Lord of the monkeys. We all know that monkeys are very fickle. It is not in their power to remain serious even for a moment. It is not in the power of any ordinary person to rule over such a race. Only the person who knows their every nerve can dominate them.

The seventh adjective is '*Raghupatipriyabhaktam*', meaning the beloved devotee of Lord Raghavendra. Hanuman is such a devotee of Rama that this couplet of Goswami Tulsidas ji is completely true for him. Even after doing such things namely tearing his heart to show that Rama resides in his heart, and crossing the ocean, he never gets arrogant.

The eighth and last adjective is '*Vaatajatam*', meaning son of the wind. Its special meaning is that just like the wind is unstoppable, Hanuman also is unstoppable. He is capable of doing all the work in every subject, area and time without any hindrance. He is capable of making his followers have unstoppable movement in the same way. The second meaning is that only that person can be successful in every field of life, who is constantly moving like the wind and does not stop.

Tulsidas ends Hanuman Chalisa with this prayer that O Hanuman! Come and settle in my heart. When Hanuman resides in his heart, Rama, Sita and Lakshman will automatically reside in his heart. One should end the recitation of Hanuman Chalisa with this final meditation of Hanuman seated in his heart and Lord Rama, Sita and Lakshman seated in Hanuman's heart. One should not aspire to serve God directly. One should aspire to serve God by serving God's servant.

By calling him Sankatharan (remover of obstacles), Tulsidas focuses on his ability to purify our intellect.

❐

# Hanuman's Management Mantra

The postgraduate degree in business management, known as Master of Business Administration (MBA), may be a lure of livelihood for the youth in the modern age, but its principles are preserved and protected in the Vedic scriptures. An efficient business manager should have the following qualities -

- Organization and time management
- Skills like problem-solving and critical thinking
- Willingness to learn
- Honesty and ethics
- Professional references
- Leadership skills
- Strong work ethics

This is the need of the hour. Let us know what management qualities were present in Hanuman ji millions of years ago-

1. Humble and enthusiastic
2. Supreme knowledge
3. Self-confident
4. Visionary
5. Statesmanship/policy expert
6. Diplomatic

7. Balanced speech
8. Truthful
9. Grateful
10. Appreciator of virtues
11. Troubleshooter
12. Skillful spy
13. Overflowing with love
14. Always ready to be tested
15. Mediator and true servant
16. Endowed with the power of fearlessness

## Humble and enthusiastic

Hanuman, the son of wind, who was blessed with humble nature, was not arrogant. He appears to be standing on the ground of reality. He always speaks the truth. He avoids lying. He does not flatter anyone. He is a nature lover. One who is a nature lover has the ability to bear every hardship in life. Such a person is a good manager. This quality is seen in Hanuman ji since childhood.

Along with Hanuman Chalisa, these qualities are also mentioned in Valmiki's Ramayana.

## Supreme knowledge

Knowledge makes a man civilized and cultured. Since ancient times, our ancestors gave special importance to knowledge and also made special arrangements for it. In today's words, a campaign was run for the distribution of knowledge. A knowledgeable man becomes more humble than before. He gets rid of ego. A source of happiness bursts forth in his heart. He remains silent and accurately evaluates every situation and circumstance and only then takes a decision. A Paramjnani never displays his knowledge. Rather, working judiciously is his motto. Our Hanuman is the ocean of knowledge. Tulsidas writes- *'Jai Hanuman Gyan Gun Sagar. Jai Kapis Tihun Lok Ujaagar.'* It is very important for a skilled manager to be knowledgeable.

### Self-confidence

The knowledgeable person is full of self-confidence. Knowledge is considered the best strength. It organizes the powers of a person. He does every difficult task easily. The work done with confidence and belief in divine power is always successful. Hanuman ji always achieves success due to this quality. On assessing the character of Hanuman ji, it is proved that he is full of self-confidence. Whatever work is assigned to him, he completes it humbly. This is a sign of his strong self-confidence and efficient administrator.

### Visionary

Enthusiasm, knowledge and self-confidence make a person visionary. A skilled manager makes his plan by examining profit-loss, fame-disgrace and other facts in deciding the policies of past, present and future. Hanuman ji moves forward after considering all the possibilities before going in search of Sita.

### Statesmanship/Policy expert

A visionary is a scholar. This has already been decided. Special guidelines are prepared for a particular work. We call them policy because a different policy is prepared for every work. This is the reason why our policy makers have written ethical things to explain to the king and the people. We all know about Vidur Niti and Chanakya Niti. The person who formulates policies using his intelligence and wisdom is called a policy expert. Hanuman ji has also been called a policy expert.

### Diplomat

Diplomacy means a nation, group or individual conducting its actions to protect its interests and maintain peaceful relations. Methods like dialogue, persuasion, compromise and pressure are used in diplomacy. Hanuman ji is also proficient in this art.

### Balanced speech

A farsighted and skilled policy director is a man of few words. He waits for the results of his policies, diplomacy and foresight to come to fruition. Depending on situations, he may remain silent or speak about. That is why he always gives a balanced speech. Hanuman ji always speaks after thinking. He answers according to the occasion. This is his efficient management. A skilled manager knows what to say, when and how much to say. This is the formula for success.

### Truthful

A person full of the above qualities is truthful. No deception. No lies. No wrong messages. This is the main message of Hanuman ji. Notice that the entire universe is rotating on the axis of truth. The path of truth may be difficult but walking on that path brings peace. Truth is never hidden and cannot be hidden.

***Satyameva jayate naanritam satyen pantha vitato devayanah.***
***Yenakramantyushayo hyaptakamo yatra tat satyasya***
***paramam nidhanam.***

(Mundaka Upanishad 3.1.6)

That is, ultimately only truth prevails and not falsehood. This is the path through which the sages, whose desires have been fulfilled, attain the ultimate goal of life. Hanuman's biography gives this message. Hanuman does not speak untruth in even a single incident. Even in adversity he speaks the truth without fear. Knowledgeable persons follow the policy of *Satyamvad dharmam chara.*

## Grateful

A person blessed with all virtues is always grateful. Such a person does not shy away from giving credit to his leader. Hanumanji also calls himself an insignificant monkey. This is his greatness. He gives credit to Shri Rama for his kindness with an open heart. This work can be done only by one who is not arrogant. This is the biggest sign of being truthful.

## Appreciator of virtues

Man is a mine of virtues and demerits. According to a story, God says that you should open the mouth of the bag containing your demerits and tightly close the mouth of the bag containing the demerits of others. Then my grace will always remain on you. In the society, that person is great who praises others from time to time after seeing their qualities. He is a virtue-grabber. He is their connoisseur. Despite being powerful, he does not show off his power but definitely praises a person when he does a good deed. From this point of view, Hanumanji is a virtue-grabber. He openly praises the qualities of others. One who gives respect to others is always proud and respected. He is praised everywhere. Hanuman gives due respect to everyone whether they are small or big.

## Troubleshooter

Tulsidas mentions in Ramcharitmanas that patience, religion, friend and wife should be tested in times of crisis. Their reality is known only in times of crisis and if there is no truth in their love, it does not take long for them to be exposed. Hanuman ji rescues his devotees selflessly from crisis at every step. He not only rescues those who are his ardent devotees but also removes the crisis of those who have come to him for the first time. Probably for this reason he has been awarded the title of Sankat Mochan.

## Skilled spy

Only a person who is a skilled spy can remove someone's crisis because he easily finds out who has created the crisis from where. To test his identity, one has to keep a close eye on his activities secretly. Hanuman ji does this to test the identity of any person and meets him by changing his form and finds out the reality. He makes his size small and big according to the time. In this way, he appears before us as a spy of the highest order. He knows all the tricks of espionage and uses them whenever required. In the Ramayana written by Valmiki and the Shri Ramcharitmanas written by Tulsidas, we are first introduced to Hanuman Ji as a spy.

## Overflowing with love

When one finds a well-wisher during espionage, every pore of his body is filled with joy. The mind and heart are overcome by love. There is no selfishness in this love. Such true love is rare.

A true lover has no expectations from the other party. Hanuman Ji is a true devotee of his Lord. He loves him from the bottom of his heart. Hanuman loves not only Rama but also his every devotee immensely.

## Always ready to be tested

A person who is infatuated is always ready for every kind of test. We see that Hanuman Ji's entire life is full of tests. He proved to be pure gold in every test. It would not be an exaggeration to say here that after passing every test, Hanuman Ji's personality kept improving. Here we learn that those who do good deeds never lose.

## Mediator and true servant

The best spy and the one who succeeds in every test is considered the best servant. This servant is capable of mediating by becoming our well-wisher. When good and bad situations arise in a person's life, only a true servant helps us. Hanuman Ji appears to be a true servant and a good mediator. Through his eloquence, intelligence, wisdom, knowledge and policy, he helps both the parties. He wants the welfare of both the parties and does only that work which is in their interest. He is not a wolf in lamb's clothing. Not only this, Hanuman does not expect anything in return for mediation.

## Enriched with the power of fearlessness

Which person will be fearless in his life? Who will be fearless? Only he will be fearless who has a strong character. Truthful, charitable, greedy, selfless, true servant and faithful Hanuman ji is endowed with the powers of fearlessness. Here we can say that Hanuman ji's fearlessness lies in his incomparable strength. In this form, he is charitable. All the above qualities should be present in an efficient manager. At present, the course of business management has been prepared according to the thinking of western countries. If Hanuman ji's management policy is implemented in the world today, then there will be efficient management in every business.

❐

# APPENDIX

## How to Please Hanuman Ji

Mangalvar (Tuesday) is the day of worship of Hanuman Ji in Kaliyug. He blesses everyone. Hanuman had also received the boon that in Kaliyug he will be worshipped on Mangalvar. Scholars believe that efforts should be made to please Hanuman Ji on Tuesday. Hanuman is a god who gets pleased very quickly because he is considered to be the incarnation of Lord Shiva. What should be done to please Hanuman Ji quickly? This question strikes the mind of every Hanuman devotee. We wish that the following efforts will fulfill all your wishes in a jiffy.

1. Hanuman Ji is the ultimate devotee of Rama. Therefore, if you want to please Hanuman Ji, then first of all please Lord Rama. Before remembering Hanuman Ji on Tuesday, make sure to bring Lord Rama's name on your tongue. Along with this, chant Rama's name 108 times daily using a rosary. Hanuman Ji will always keep his blessings on you.

2. If you want to enjoy material comforts in life, then offer red vermilion to Hanuman, the son of wind, on Tuesday. Doing this gives Rajyoga. All the sorrows of life are removed. Happiness comes in life. We enjoy many kinds of happiness.

3. Getting Sundarkand recited at home on Tuesday is also considered beneficial. This strengthens the financial

condition of the house. All the negative energy of the house is eliminated by this recitation. Happiness and peace remain in the house. There are no fights. The family progresses.

4. Keeping a fast in the name of Hanuman ji on Tuesday is also a great solution. On this day, do not eat anything, but feed the poor or needy persons. Bajrang Bali will be happy to see your generosity. He will fulfill your desired wish. He will keep your house blessed.
5. If you are troubled by bad dreams at night, then keep alum near Hanuman ji for some time on Tuesday. Then remove this alum from yourself and throw it in a deserted area. You will stop getting bad dreams.
6. If your house is haunted by evil spirits or ghosts, then start reciting Hanuman Chalisa every Tuesday or every day. This will prevent any kind of evil spirits from wandering around your house.
7. Ram Raksha Stotra should be recited on Tuesday. This makes Lord Hanuman happy. He protects you. Even the enemy cannot conquer you. Nothing bad will happen to you.
8. It is considered auspicious to feed gram or any fruit to a monkey on Tuesday. While doing this, remember Lord Hanuman and say any wish of yours. It will be fulfilled soon.

❐

# The Tallest Hanuman Statues

Hanuman, an ardent devotee of Lord Rama, devoted his entire life to the service of Lord Rama and Sita. Today, he is admired and worshipped all over the world as a symbol of loyalty, strength and devotion. Apart from Hanuman temples, there are many tall Hanuman statues standing proudly in India. These statues fascinate the devotees.

## 1. Panchamukhi Anjaneya Swamy Statue, Karnataka

The Panchamukhi Anjaneya Swamy statue located in Bidnagere Basaveshwara Math in Karnataka stands at a remarkable height of 161 feet. Made with intricate details and shining like gold, this statue is a real delight to look at. It has five faces representing the various incarnations of Lord Hanuman i.e., Hayagriva, Garuda, Narasimha, Varaha. It has ten arms. These arms hold important symbols like conch, trident, sword, shield, mace and axe.

## 2. Jakhu Temple Statue, Himachal Pradesh

Tucked amidst the hills of Shimla, the capital of Himachal Pradesh, lies the Jakhu Temple. It houses a 108-feet tall statue of Lord Hanuman. The Lord greets with a warm smile. Built in bright orange and golden colours, the statue holds a special place in the hearts of devotees as it is believed to be the place where Lord Hanuman rested during his search for the Sanjivani herb.

## 3. Sankat Mochan Hanuman Temple, Delhi

Sankat Mochan Hanuman stands as a true masterpiece that radiates positive and peaceful energy. The iconic statue within the temple complex depicts Lord Hanuman ripping open his chest so that Lord Rama, Mata Sita and brother Lakshman can reside in his heart. A symbol of unwavering devotion, it has been a revered landmark of the city for centuries. The temple that houses the statue is an ancient marvel standing since the 18th century.

## 4. Nalco Temple, Odisha

The 108.9 feet tall statue of Lord Hanuman stands proudly at the NalcoTemple in the serene town of Damanjodi in Odisha. One hand is raised in Abhaya Mudra, assuring protection from all evil forces. The other hand is holding a powerful mace. The color of the statue is pure white which adds to its overall beauty.

## 5. Paritala Anjaneya Temple, Andhra Pradesh

The magnificent statue of Hanuman is located at the Paritala Anjaneya Temple in Andhra Pradesh. It is 135 feet tall. The statue of Veer Abhaya Anjaneya Hanuman Swamy is the tallest and largest Hanuman statue in the world. The statue of Abhaya Anjaneya Hanuman was installed in the year 2003.

## 6. Madapam, Andhra Pradesh

India's tallest and largest Hanuman statue is installed on the banks of the Vamsadhara River in Srikakulam district of Andhra Pradesh. It is a 176 feet tall statue.

## 7. Nandura, Maharashtra

You will find a magnificent statue made of marble along the National Highway 6 in Maharashtra. This 105 feet tall statue of Lord Hanuman blesses all the travellers who set out on the yatra. The statue is of a beautiful white colour and has colourful garlands around its neck with a hint of gold.

### 8. Hanumat Dham, Shahjahanpur, Uttar Pradesh

Situated at Birasat Ghat on the banks of the Khannaut River in Uttar Pradesh, Hanumat Dham houses a 100 feet tall magnificent statue of Lord Hanuman. Standing on a 25 feet high platform, the statue is a treat to the eyes. Walking around the serene environment of the ghat, you will feel a sense of peace in your heart amidst the presence of Lord Hanuman.

### 9. Agara, Karnataka

The Hanuman temple at Agara in the bustling city of Bangalore is adorned with a 102 feet tall lifelike statue of Bajrangbali. Dressed in colourful royal attires the deity stands as a symbol of strength and protection. It is considered as one of the most beautiful attractions in Bangalore.

### 10. Chhatarpur, Delhi

The hundred-foot statue of Hanuman is located in the Chhatarpur area of the capital Delhi. Painted in bright orange, this statue stands as a ray of hope and salvation. Located in the temple premises, this statue provides solace and shelter to the devotees who seek the blessings of Sankat Mochan.

❐

# The Glory of the Name of Bajrangbali

Bajrangbali (common name for the Hindu deity Hanuman) is the giver of eight siddhis and nine niddhis (treasures). It is said that the glory of the 12 names of Bajrangbali is boundless. These names are the symbols of happiness, prosperity, wealth, goodwill, beauty, courage and solutions. It is mentioned in mythological texts that Kesari Nandan Hanuman gives the best result of worship in Kaliyug.

Hanuman who accomplishes the tasks of Lord Rama is the incarnation of Rudra himself. He is the troubleshooter. His strength is used in accomplishing the tasks of others and removing sorrows. At present, the Siddha Purushas who have accomplished the siddhis of Hanuman Ji are of the opinion that if Mahabali Pawan Putra is worshipped with a true heart, then he fulfills every wish of his devotee. Hanuman Ji has many names. By whatever name the devotee calls him, he comes running to remove the troubles of the devotee.

There is a religious belief in Indian society that by merely taking the name of Hanuman ji, the devotee gets everything like wealth, property, knowledge, health, prosperity, child and much more. By properly worshipping Hanuman ji, one gets good results soon.

In Kaliyug, Rama devotee Hanuman is the most proven god. Remembering the twelve names of Hanuman ji is extremely beneficial. Chanting the names of Hanuman ji removes all problems. At present, debt and illness are the two biggest problems in front of every human being. Debt means to return the money taken from people and illness means ill-health.

Regular recitation of the following 12 names of Hanuman ji is considered best. These are: Hanuman, Anjanisut, Vayuputra, Mahabal, Ramesht, Phalgunasakha, Pingaksha, Amitavikram, Uddhikraman, Sitoshokavinashan, Laxmanpraanadata and Dashagrivadarpaha. Each name has its own glory.

According to scholars, reciting the 12 names of Hanuman ji in the morning is considered good. By taking these names in the morning, a person lives a long life. By taking these names in the afternoon, one becomes rich. After this, one should remember these names once again before sleeping at night. By taking these names at night, opponents are defeated and enemies are pacified. Before starting a new work, it is said that pronouncing the twelve names of Hanuman ji is the best. One should also remember them before starting a journey.

Another remedy is also suggested. Write 12 names of Hanuman ji in red color on a yellow paper. These names can also be put at the main entrance of the house and the place of worship. By writing it with Ashtagandha on Bhojpatra, it can be worn around the neck like a locket. Wearing it in a silver or copper locket not only gives freedom from fear but also increases the self-confidence of the person wearing it. By using these names, a person is protected from all ten directions.

**Jai Bajrangbali!**

❑❑❑